ANCIENT MONUMENTS
REVEALED

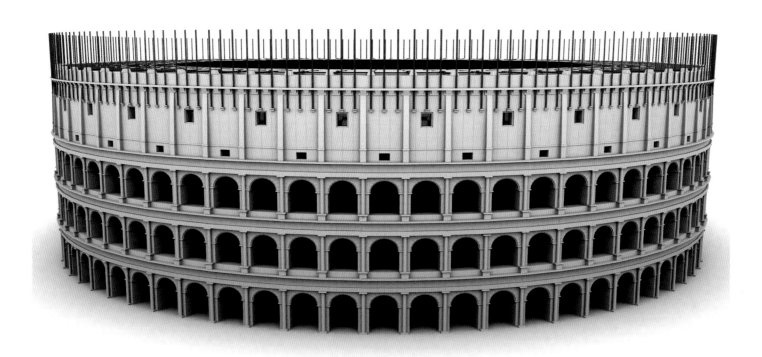

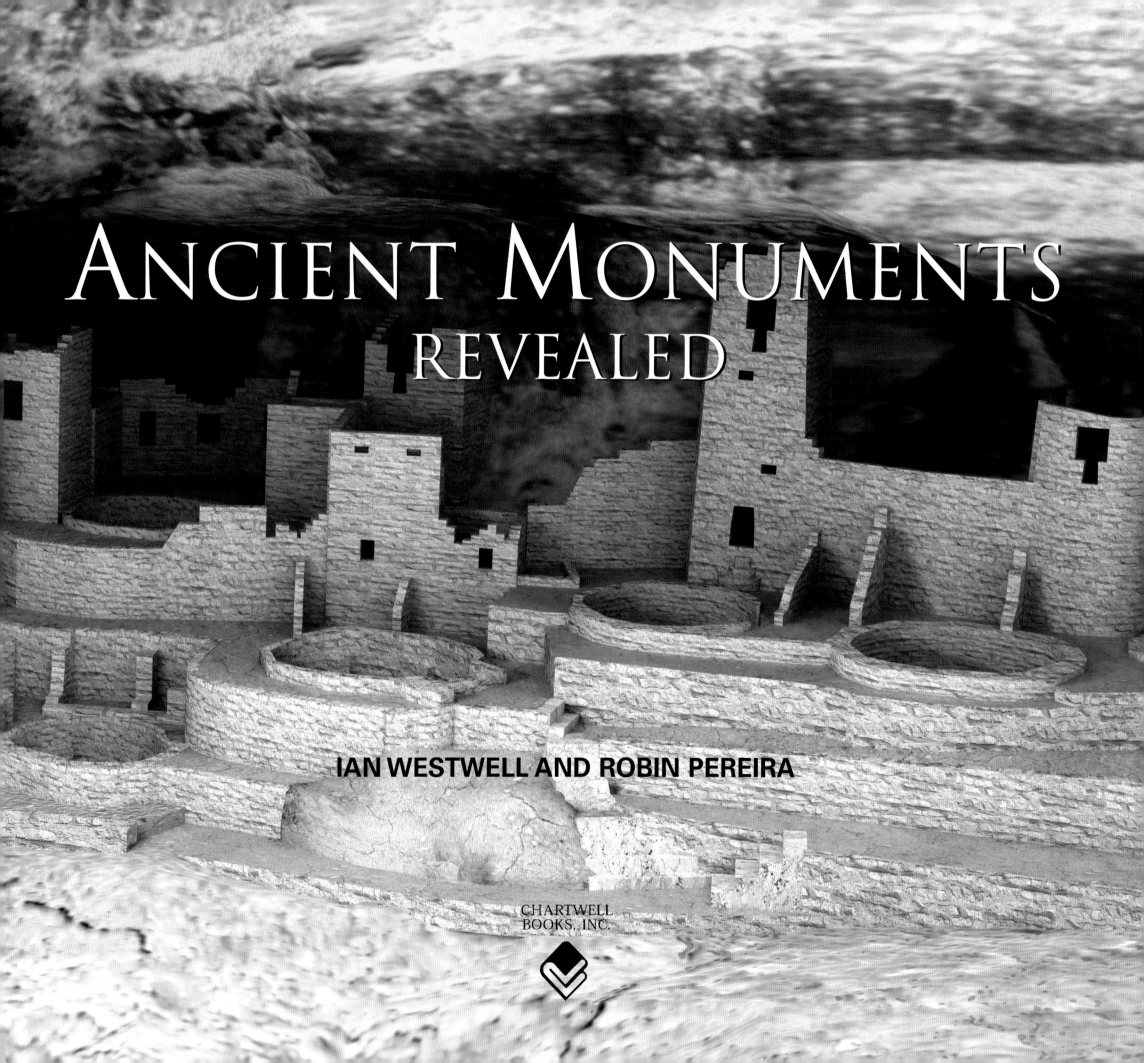

ANCIENT MONUMENTS
REVEALED

IAN WESTWELL AND ROBIN PEREIRA

CHARTWELL
BOOKS, INC.

This edition published by:

CHARTWELL BOOKS, INC.
A Division of
BOOK SALES, INC.
114 Northfield Avenue
Edison, New Jersey 08837

ISBN—13: 978—0—7858—2080—2
ISBN—10: 0—7858—2080—9

© 2006 by Compendium Publishing Ltd.,
43 Frith Street, London W1D 4SA,
United Kingdom

Cataloging-in-Publication data is available from
the Library of Congress

Designer: Dave Ball

Color reproduction: anorax

Printed in: China

PAGE 1: *The Colosseum—also spelled
Coliseum and also called the Flavian
Amphitheater—in Rome. See Chapter IV.*

PAGES 2/3: *The breathtaking Mesa Verde—see
Chapter V.*

RIGHT: *Statue in front of the ruins of the
Temple of the Warriors, Chichen Itza. See
Chapter VI.*

FAR RIGHT: *The Erechtheion was built in
around 406 B.C. It is most famous for the
Caryatids (seen here) on the southern porch
side of the building. See page 86 for more
details.*

CONTENTS

INTRODUCTION
PAGE 6

CHAPTER I
THE PYRAMIDS
PAGE 14

CHAPTER II
TEOTIHUACAN
PAGE 36

CHAPTER III
THE ACROPOLIS
PAGE 58

CHAPTER IV
THE COLOSSEUM
PAGE 86

CHAPTER V
MESA VERDE
PAGE 110

CHAPTER VI
CHICHEN ITZA
PAGE 134

PHOTO CREDITS
PAGE 160

INTRODUCTION

INTRODUCTION

Although the modern world is awash with recently built monumental structures of one kind or another, humans down the ages have always striven to create such sites despite their comparative technical backwardness compared with the builders and architects of the present. While modern man can rely on all types of powerful mechanical devices to aid construction work, the earliest builders had to rely on nothing more than pulleys, levers, ramps, and above all, muscle power to build their creations. Some even lacked that most crucial piece of technology, the wheel.

Nor could they make use of all the modern materials available to today's architects; they largely had to make do with stone, brick, and wood. Yet despite all of these potential limitations to their construction skills, they still managed to perform feats of structural engineering that remain awe-inspiring even to the people of today. This book looks at six such structures—three of them are from the pre-Columbian Americas, two from the European Classical world of the Greek and Romans, and one is from the ancient Egyptian world.

These sites were variously places of religious worship or ceremonial significance, homes to both the powerful and lowly or places of sometimes lethal entertainment. Some combined several functions at the same time, while the role of others changed as the years passed by. The Acropolis, for instance, has variously been a pagan religious center, a place of Muslim and Christian worship, and a military headquarters or fortress. Three of the sites—all in the Americas—were cities of various sizes; two were largely religious complexes, while one was a place of bloody entertainment for the masses. In some cases archaeologists and historians have uncovered the history of the people who built or lived in and around these structures but in some cases they know comparatively little as the original inhabitants left no written record of either their lives or cultures. We even know very

ABOVE AND RIGHT: *The Great Pyramid at Giza is the only surviving member of the Seven Ancient Wonders of the World. The pyramids were built near the ancient Egyptian capital city of Memphis for the fourth dynasty kings Khufu, Khafre, and Menkaure. The largest pyramid is the Great Pyramid of Khufu and built to entomb the remains of the great pharaoh who ruled Egypt between about 2,589 and 2,566 B.C.*

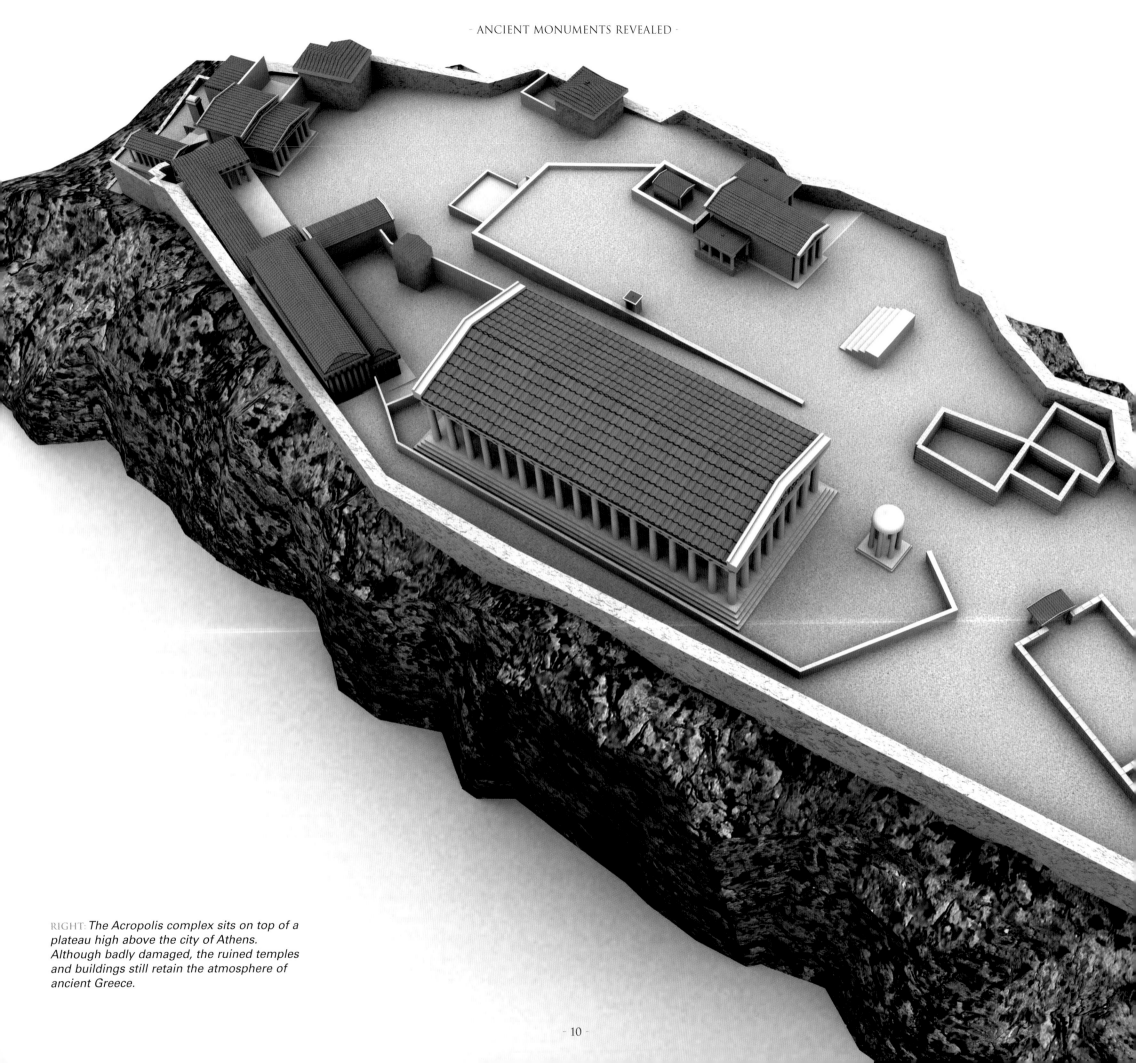

RIGHT: *The Acropolis complex sits on top of a plateau high above the city of Athens. Although badly damaged, the ruined temples and buildings still retain the atmosphere of ancient Greece.*

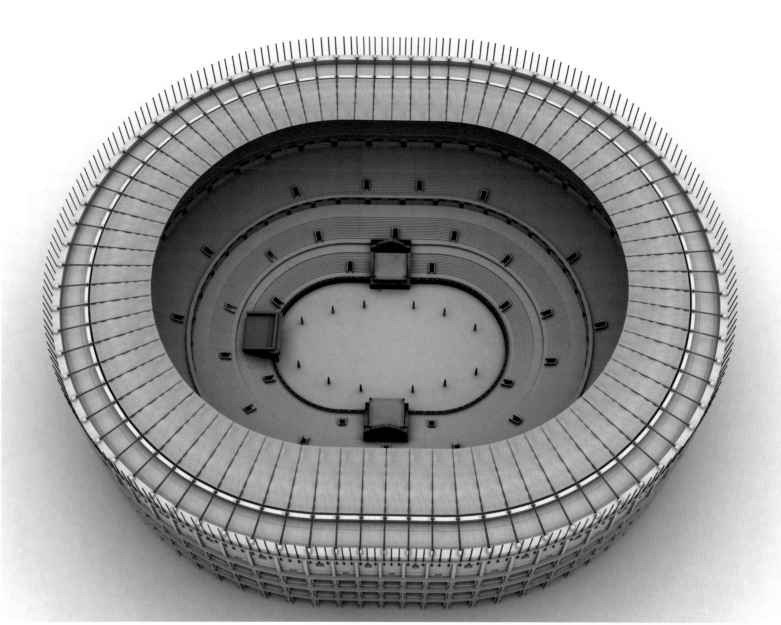

little about their architects, the probably thousands of skilled and unskilled laborers who worked on them, or indeed the various artists who decorated them in an often lavish style.

The structures discussed in this book are, in a descending order of antiquity, first the pyramids of Giza and the other structures associated with them that were built by the kings of ancient Egypt's Fourth Dynasty, which flourished between 2613–2494 B.C. The second feat of pre-industrial civil engineering is the heart of a pre-Columbian city-state founded in what is now south-central Mexico. This is Teotihuacan, a city of around 150,000 or more people at its height located to the north of modern Mexico City. It was first settled between 600 and 200 B.C. and flourished until around 750 B.C. and the various stepped pyramids built by the original inhabitants in its heyday rival those found at Giza. Next comes the magnificent Acropolis, the ceremonial and religious heart of the ancient Greek city-state of Athens. Its most magnificent buildings, including the Parthenon, were constructed during the period 490–415 B.C.

The fourth edifice is the Colosseum in Rome, one of the empire's most imposing structures, yet one deeply stained in the blood of both humans and animals. Work began in A.D. 72 and the amphitheater was used for spectacles of various sorts until the early sixth century A.D. The penultimate masterpiece of engineering takes us to what is today the United States. The subjects are the many stone and adobe buildings found in the Mesa Verde National Park in Colorado. These impressive often multi-story structures, many of which are situated high up in cliff recesses, were built by the Anasazi Native American people, who flourished in the area between A.D. 500–c.1250. The final subject returns the reader to pre-Colombian Mexico. It is another outstanding cityscape, one that matches the beauty of Teotihuacan. Chichen Itza was first settled in around A.D. 700 and the city-state held a dominant position on Mexico's Yucatan Peninsula

ABOVE: *Teotihuacan, the City of the Gods, is an ancient Mesoamerican city in Mexico that is still being dug out of the thick jungle that has smothered and hidden it for centuries.*

RIGHT: *The ancient ruins of Chichen Itza are located on the Yucatan Peninsula in Mexico and were built by the Mayan civilization.*

until about 1200, when its power and influence ebbed away.

The various structures were produced by largely different cultures that had for the most part no contact with each other— although there were clearly Greek influences on the architecture of the Roman Colosseum—but the various structures share some common traits. Not least is that all were built predominantly from stone, and in several cases—the Pyramids, the Acropolis, and the Colosseum—the preferred choice was limestone. This was partly due to the fact that it was found close or not too far away from the construction site, but was also due to the very nature of the stone itself.

Limestone is a sedimentary rock that contains at least 50 percent calcium carbonate and is made up organic material, such as the remains of shells or coral. It is generally easier to work that other types of

rock, particularly harder igneous and metamorphic ones such as granite and marble, the later being limestone transformed by great heat and pressure. Limestone does, however, have a great weakness and one that threatens the future of some of these ancient structures: It is ready soluble in water that contains carbon dioxide—what today is more commonly known as acid rain, much of which is generated by the internal combustion engine. Both the Colosseum and the Acropolis, the latter in particular, are being ravaged by this form of pollution. Many of the latter's surviving carvings have been removed from the open air and housed under cover to prevent their delicate scenes from crumbling away further.

None of the structures that remain today have escaped the ravages of time, and most have suffered greatly at the hand

of man, either deliberately or through simple neglect. The pyramids of Giza, the Acropolis, and the Colosseum have all had their limestone blocks looted for other building projects at various times. In some cases their great treasures have either been stolen or removed elsewhere to protect them on sometimes dubious legal grounds. Both of these are certainly true in the case of the pyramids and the latter, although it remains a contentious issue, is arguably true of the Acropolis. Some have suffered the impact of earthquakes (the pyramids and the Colosseum), explosions (the Acropolis), and fire (Teotihuacan) but none has been entirely been lost to the modern world. Although they have been much abused by both humankind and nature until the very recent past, their grandeur remains largely undimmed.

Today all of these great structures are to a lesser or greater degree protected by their country's governments and the visiting public have been barred from walking through or clambering over all or parts of the sites. Nevertheless vital conservation and preservation efforts are ongoing at all the structures to save them for future generations.

ABOVE: *Cliff Palace is one of a series of extraordinary cliff dwellings in Mesa Verde, Colorado and was constructed by ancient Pueblo peoples who then soon mysteriously abandoned them.*

CHAPTER I
THE PYRAMIDS

THE PYRAMIDS

THE OLDEST SURVIVING EXAMPLE OF THE SEVEN ANCIENT WONDERS

ABOVE: *Locator map–Giza is in northeast Egypt.*

PREVIOUS PAGE: *The pyramids today.*

RIGHT: *The Giza plateau is part of the necropolis of ancient Memphis. Originally all three of the big pyramids at Giza had causeways, valley temples, and mortuary temples. These structures were originally faced with smoother and harder limestone or granite that was partly or entirely stripped in ancient and medieval times, leaving limestone core blocks that have weathered over the years.*

There were once Seven Wonders* of the World but today only one of them, the ancient Egyptian pyramids at Giza to the west of Cairo, survive. These monumental structures were, in fact, each the heart of a larger complex of buildings that included other, smaller pyramids, mortuary temples, ceremonial boat pits, causeways, and of course, the enigmatic Sphinx.

The three pyramids that are at the heart of Giza were constructed at the command of three kings of ancient Egypt's Fourth Dynasty (2613–2494 B.C.)—Khufu (Greek name Cheops), Khafre (Chephren), and Menkaure (Mykerinos). Their intention was to not only build their own final resting places but also to make them places of eternal worship. The pyramids, which are just two miles (3km) from Giza, are all associated with other structures. Each of the three rulers built a pyramid temple on his pyramid's east side and had a causeway connecting his tomb to a valley temple even farther to the east. Other structures,

* The Seven Wonders of the Ancient World were:
• Great Pyramid at Giza
• Hanging Gardens of Babylon
• Statue of Zeus at Olympia
• Temple of Artemis at Ephesus
• Mausoleum of King Maussollos at Halicarnassus
• Colossus of Rhodes
• Pharos (lighthouse) at Alexandria

including smaller pyramids and mastaba (see below) were generally reserved for senior members of the royal family and important court officials. Those administrators and religious officials who ran the pyramid complexes or performed religious ceremonies in them were housed in villages close to the various temples.

BUILDING THE PYRAMIDS

The large pyramids were an immense undertaking—Khufu's Great Pyramid alone needed two million blocks of limestone—and this is reflected in their heights. Khufu's pyramid rises to 486 feet (148m), that of Khafre to 476 feet (145m), although it appears greater because it was built on higher ground, and that of Menkaure 220 feet (67m). They were originally clad in gleaming white Tura limestone but most of this was removed after A.D. 1212 to carry out repair work in Cairo after a major earthquake. The pyramids are remarkable feats of ancient engineering. The Great Pyramid, for example, has sides aligned almost exactly due north, its base is very nearly absolutely level, while its four sides are almost identical in length, varying by as little as 3 inches (7.5cm). The stone blocks were so finally hewn by the masons that there are no discernible gaps between them.

There is plenty of evidence to show how the construction work was carried out. The ancient Egyptians were not short of either unskilled or skilled labor and the

tools at hand, mostly made from bronze, stone, and wood, were equal to the task. Most of the rough-hewn blocks were sourced from quarries in the vicinity of Giza and, once rough-cut from the bed rock, they were then moved to the site by barge, sled, and rollers. Once the blocks had arrived, masons set to work dressing them, ensuring that they were the correct size and shape for their final position. They were measured using simple lengths of rope and then worked to the correct size using chisels and hammers. Simple levels insured that the work was accurate. Next the dressed blocks were moved to where they were needed. They were pulled up ramps; they were raised by ropes and lifting devices; or they were simply levered into position.

INSIDE THE GREAT PYRAMID

Although the interior organization of the pyramids vary, they do contain similar elements. In the case of the Great Pyramid, entry was by way of an opening on its north face some 55 feet (17m) above ground. Then a low, narrow corridor descends at an angle of 26 degrees until it hits the bedrock before continuing downward for nearly 100 feet (30.5m) at which point it levels out. This horizontal passage runs for a further 30 feet (9.1m) or so and leads to what is known as the Subterranean Chamber. This measures 46 feet (14m) by 27 feet 1 inch (8.3m) and is

THIS PAGE: *The pyramid of Khufu is the largest of the three principal pyramids on the Giza Plateau. It was built for the pharaoh Khufu (Greek name Cheops) who reigned 2551–2528 B.C. The other two pyramids are those of Khafre (Chephren, 2520–2494 B.C.) and Menkaure (Mycerinus, 2490–2472 B.C.) All were kings of the fourth dynasty.*

11 feet 6 inches (3.5m) high. Archaeologists believe that a square pit in the floor indicates that the chamber was never finished. The reasons for its unfinished state remain a matter of debate as does the thought process behind an extremely confined (and equally unfinished) horizontal corridor that begins in the chamber's southern corner.

A second equally confined but ascending passage leads off the one that descends to the Subterranean Chamber and has a near identical slope. This runs for some 130 feet (39.6m) before reaching another—but horizontal—corridor that leads to the so-called Queen's Chamber. The name bears no relation to its real function and was mistakenly given to the chamber by the early Arabs who explored the site. The chamber was built on the pyramid's exact central east-to-west axis and measures some 19 feet (5.8m) by 17 feet (5.2m) and is around 15 feet (4.6m) high. The builders carved a deep niche into the chamber's east wall, possibly to house a statue of the departed king. Although the walls and ceiling are expertly finished, the floor appears to have been left unfinished. What is clear is that the work ended when the chamber was sealed by blocking off the entrance corridor where it meets the ascending corridor.

The ascending corridor finally leads to the pyramid's most impressive internal spaces—the Grand Gallery and the King's

RIGHT: *Though the pyramids are the most famous monuments at Giza, the site has been a necropolis almost from the beginning of Pharaonic Egypt. A tomb just on the outskirts of the Giza site dates from the reign of the First Dynasty Pharaoh Wadj (Djet), and discoveries in a tomb in the southern part of Giza mention the Second Dynasty Pharaoh Ninetjer. Many of the old tombs were filled in or destroyed to build the Great Pyramids. Khufu's is the largest in Egypt, topping the Red Pyramid at Dahshur built by his father Snefru by 30ft (10m). Top to bottom: The Great Pyramid of Khufu, the Pyramid of Khafre, and the Pyramid of Menkaure.*

ABOVE: *Mastaba entrance against the pyramid of Khufu. The jagged edges of the pyramid reveal the lack of the original smooth veneer of fine limestone. This exterior stone was "quarried" away through the centuries to be used in other building projects.*

LEFT: *The smallest of the three pyramids is that of Khafre's son, Menkaure. It is not entirely of limestone—the top is of brick. One theory explaining this is that Menkaure died before his pyramid could be completed, and the remaining construction was hastily done to finish it in time for the burial. It is also not exactly along a diagonal line that runs through the Great Pyramid and Khafre's, but is some 300ft (100m) to the southeast. Some say that this puts the three pyramids into an alignment resembling that of the three "belt" stars in the constellation Orion: Alnitak, Alnilam, and Mintaka.*

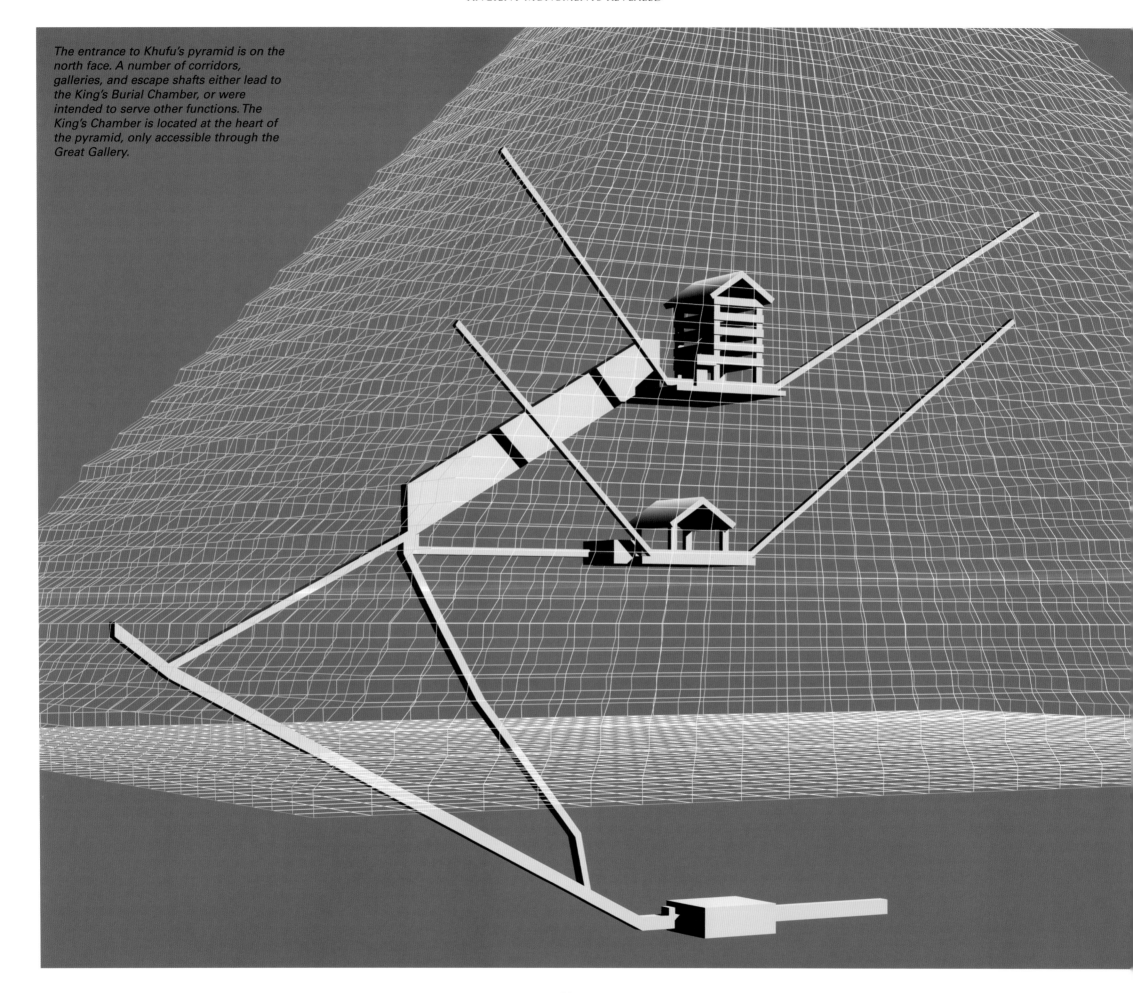

The entrance to Khufu's pyramid is on the north face. A number of corridors, galleries, and escape shafts either lead to the King's Burial Chamber, or were intended to serve other functions. The King's Chamber is located at the heart of the pyramid, only accessible through the Great Gallery.

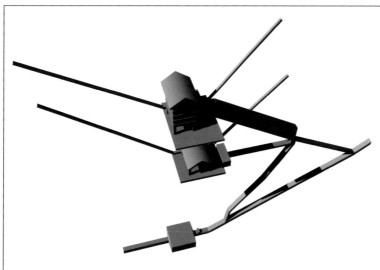

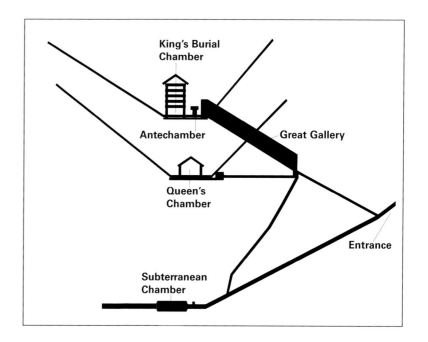

King's Burial
Chamber

Antechamber

Great Gallery

Queen's
Chamber

Entrance

Subterranean
Chamber

ABOVE, RIGHT, AND BELOW: *Three views of the passageways inside Khufu's pyramid.*

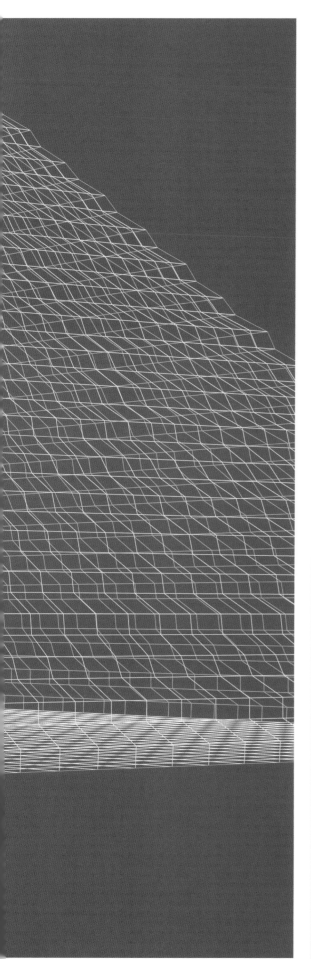

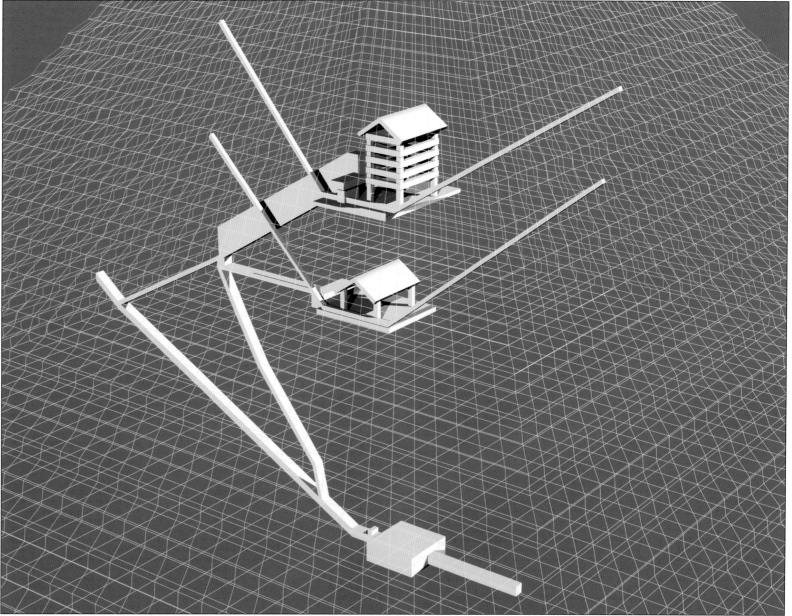

Burial Chamber. The former is in stark contrast to the confined corridor that must be climbed to reach it. It is a staggering 153 feet (46.6m) long and has a height of 28 feet (8.5m). The lower part of the walls consist of highly polished limestone and thereafter they are made from seven courses of stone mounted one above the other, but with each protruding 3 inches (7.6 cm) more than its predecessor. When the roof, which consists of several carefully laid slabs, is reached there is just 3 feet 5 inches (102.7cm) between the walls. The floor also has a interesting design. There is a 2-foot (60cm) high, 1-foot 8-inches (50cm) wide platform running along the entire length of the foot of each wall and these are separated by a trough that exactly mirrors the distance between the walls when they reach the roof.

The Grand Gallery is also embellished with a number of equally spaced and regularly sized holes that have been cut into the platform and the lower walls. There are two parallel rows of 27and two others at the step that leads from the Grand Gallery into the Antechamber to the King's Tomb, making 56 holes in total. Another feature begins in the chamber. This lies at the end of the ramp on the chamber's western side and consists of a small straight shaft that descends through the heart of the pyramid before angling off into the bedrock where it emerges into the descending passageway that leads to the previously mentioned Subterranean Chamber. Three of the Antechamber's walls, those lying to the east, south and west, were built out of red granite and there are four large slots cut into the east and west walls, with one of them being somewhat smaller than the other three.

The King's Chamber was constructed from the same red granite as the Antechamber but is a much bigger space. It

measure some 34 feet 4 inches (10.5m) by 17 feet 2 inches (5.2m) and is 19 feet 1 inch (5.8m) high. A granite sarcophagus lies near the west wall and it lies precisely on the pyramid's central axis. It was the final resting place of Khufu but the lid and the wooden coffin that once lay inside are long gone, taken or smashed by tomb raiders. The roof consists of nine huge slabs, which in total weigh around 400 tonnes. Because of the huge load bearing down on the roof, the builders created a number of other chambers above the KIng's to help lessen the immense pressure. Four of these chambers are flat and rectangular while the fifth is pitched like a modern house roof. Archaeologists have found graffiti on some of the limestone blocks in the chambers and one reveals the pride that the ordinary workers felt while building the pyramids. One line reads; "We did this with pride in the name of our Great King Khufu."

Both the King's and Queen's Chambers also contain small angled shafts. In the former case, two begin about three feet (90cm) above ground level on opposite walls and shoot upwards to the exterior of the pyramid at an angle of either 31 degrees (north wall) or 45 degrees (south wall). The former is orientated to the Pole Star, while the latter is fixed on the constellation of Orion. Similar shafts have been discovered in the Queen's Chamber. Both are orientated in a similar way to those in the King's Chamber but they do not reach the exterior of the pyramid. It was discovered that the southern shaft was blocked by a stone plug fixed with two copper pins at around 214 feet (65m). Archaeologists accept that these shafts were for ritual purposes but no one is sure why those in the Queen's Chamber were blocked off.

All of the three main pyramids were designed to prevent the king's mummy and the symbolic and practical goods buried with his remains from being looted by grave robbers. The means of doing this varied for each pyramid but basically involved a series of stone portcullises,

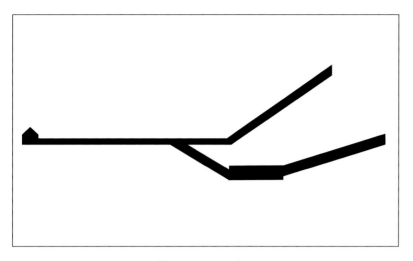

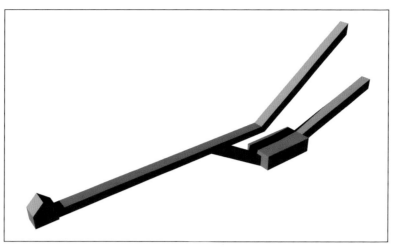

ABOVE, RIGHT, AND BELOW: *Three views of the passageways inside Khafre's pyramid.*

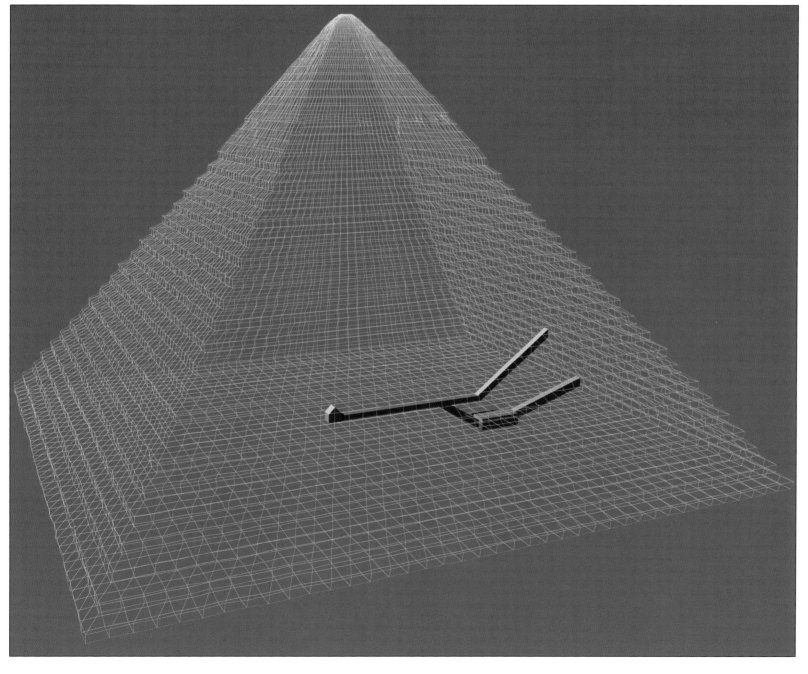

large stone blocks, and concealed entrances. Yet none of these measures prevented wholesale looting. Archaeologists believe that Khufu's Great Pyramid was all but emptied by around 2150 B.C. and the others suffered a similar fate. However the tomb raiders did not strip everything out of the tombs as some objects were effectively immovable. As mentioned Khufu's unfinished granite sarcophagus remains in place as does the finished sarcophagus of Khafre. Menkaure's granite sarcophagus was removed by the British in the mid-nineteenth century but was lost at sea, although his wooden coffin did make it to the British Museum.

GIZA'S OTHER EGYPTIAN TREASURES

Khufu's pyramid, like the two others, was part of a larger complex that consisted of various structures. The pyramid was once surrounded by a 26 foot (8m) high wall also made from Tura limestone that bordered a courtyard-type feature some 33 feet (10m) wide. Admittance to this was by way of a doorway at the northwest corner of an associated mortuary temple that once stood on the eastern side of the pyramid. This was rectilinear in shape, measuring 171 feet (52m) on its longest, north-south axis and measured 132 feet (40m) from east to west. Like the pyramid it, too, was built out of limestone and was decorated with ornate reliefs. The roof of the main structure was supported by square and oblong granite columns and the interior consisted of a large cloistered courtyard that was open to the skies and paved with black basalt. Access to the roof was by way of a stone staircase located at the temple's southwest corner. There was a significant recess on the western side of the mortuary temple that gave way to a further enclosure, one possibly used for storage. There was also an inner sanctuary that, according to some though not all Egyptologists, contained an altar flanked by engraved, round-topped stone columns.

The site also has several so-called boat pits. These neatly fall into two

ABOVE AND RIGHT: *The Giza necropolis gets bigger as excavations find new tombs and artifacts—it has come a long way since Bezoni, Caviglia, Perring, and Vyse began the first systematic study in the early 1800s.*

DIMENSIONS

THE GREAT PYRAMID OF KHUFU	• **Height:** 146.5m • **Base:** 23.38m • **Slope:** 51° 50'
GREAT GALLERY	• **Height:** 8.48 to 8.74m • **Length:** 47.85m • **Slope:** 26° 16' 40"
QUEEN'S CHAMBER	• **Height** 6.26m • **Length:** 5.76m • **Width:** 5.23m
KING'S CHAMBER	• **Height:** 5.84m • **Length:** 1.49m • **Width:** 5.42m
CAUSEWAY	• **Length:** 825m
BOAT PITS (ON NE AND SE CORNERS)	• **Depth:** 8m • **Length:** 52m • **Width:** 7.5m
PYRAMID OF KHAFRE	• **Height:** 147.3m • **Base:** 215.25m • **Slope:** 53° 10'
CAUSEWAY	• **Length:** 494.6m
CULT PYRAMID	• **Base:** 29m • **Slope:** 53° 54'
PYRAMID OF MENKAURE	• **Height:** 66.45m • **Base:** 104.6m • **Slope:** 51° 20'
CAUSEWAY	• **Length:** 608m
PYRAMID G 1-a	• **Height:** 28.4m • **Base:** 44m • **Slope:** 52° 15'
PYRAMID G 1-b	• **Height:** 28.4m • **Base:** 31.24m • **Slope:** 52° 15'
PYRAMID G 1-c	• **Height:** 28.4m • **Base:** 31.24m • **Slope:** 52° 15'

categories—some were merely dug in the shape of a boat and the others, usually long rectangular pits, actually contained all the parts needed to reassemble a fully-functioning boat. Archaeologists have uncovered five separate groups of boats. The first lies around the pyramid outside its enclosing wall. Another was positioned close to the mortuary temple, roughly parallel to the Causeway (see below). This was the last such group to be discovered. The two pits were found by local Egyptologist Kamal el-Mallakh in May 1954 and his workers had to remove large blocks of limestone to gain access to them. The first pit contained more than 1,220 individual items of boat that were eventually reassembled by a team working under Hag Ahmed Yusuf. It took 14 years to complete the task, putting together pieces of wood that varied in size from as little as 4 inches (10cm) to 75 feet (23m), and the restored vessel can now be seen at the Giza Museum. It is a staggering 142 feet (43.3m) long and displaced around 45 tons. The three other groups lie to the north and south of the mortuary temple, another can be found between two of the Queens' Pyramids and the fifth is associated with the Satellite Pyramid.

The latter is a smaller facsimile of Khufu's own pyramid and it is located directly to the southeast of the larger structure. The sides of its base are a mere fraction of its larger cousin, measuring just 66 feet (20 m). Archaeologists are not entirely sure what the pyramid was actually built for but most believe it was related to the larger pyramid. Some have suggested that it was constructed to house Khufu's ka, which was the personality double the ancient Egyptians believed that they were born with and after their death lived on in a statue of the deceased. Whatever the case the Satellite Pyramid has a sloping T-shaped passage that is associated with a small burial chamber.

The complex also contains the three Queens' Pyramids built under the orders of Khufu at 90 degrees to the upper reaches of the Causeway on the southeast corner

of the Great Pyramid. The three structures have been prosaically christened GI-a, GI-b and GI-c by archaeologists and, although much smaller, they in part mimic the Great Pyramid. They were once associated with smaller versions of the latter's mortuary temple and each contains a burial chamber that is accessed by a descending passage that takes a sharp turn to the west before the chamber proper is reached. It is believed that these pyramids were built for three queens. The first, the most northerly, was probably created for Queen Hetepheres, who in all likelihood was the mother of Khufu. The next was probably built to house Queen Meritetes, who may have been the wife who bore Khufu's eldest son, Kawab. The final pyramid in the group has been linked to Queen Henutsen, who may have been half-sister to Khufu.

The next structure of note was the Causeway, a corridor that linked the main complex of buildings with the so-called Valley Temple and ran a little to the north of the Queens' Pyramids. Little of the Valley Temple remains in situ apart from some basalt paving and archaeologists are undecided as to the precise look of the complex. The Causeway itself is better preserved, although the lower end has been swallowed up by the spread of the comparatively recent town of Kafr es-Samman. The structure was undoubtedly another major building project as at some points the foundations rose to more than 130 feet (40m) above the surrounding terrain, while at other points the corridor was built directly over the area's bed rock. It appears from fragments found among the remains of the Causeway that it was decorated with intricate carvings of animals.

There are also two extensive cemeteries to the west and east of the Great Pyramid. The various tombs are known as mastabas, which Egyptologists define as a rectangular stone building that is connect to a mummy chamber in the underlying rock. In both cases the mastabas are neatly arranged in parallel rows with each separated from its

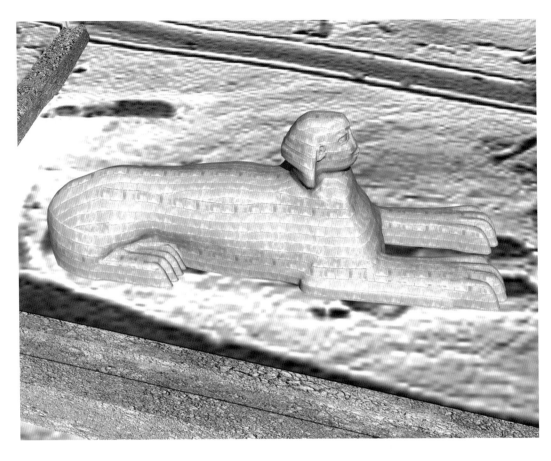

neighbour by several feet. When the mastabas were built they would have been encased in the same limestone that once covered the pyramids. It is thought that the eastern cemetery contained the remains of the king's relatives, while that to the west was reserved for important court officials.

THE SPHINX

The final structure of the Giza complex is probably as well known as the Great Pyramid itself but the two are in fact in no way connected despite their close proximity. The Sphinx, the imposing sculpture of a lion with the face of a man, was not, as many people assume, built by Khufu but was constructed some time after his death by Khafre as part of his own pyramid complex. Khafre was the younger sibling of Djedefre, Khufu's successor who ruled only briefly from 2528 B.C. to 2520 B.C. Khafre came to the throne when the latter died and ruled until 2494 B.C. He ordered the Sphinx to be carved out of the underlying rock in the years before 2500 B.C. and when the work was completed the crouching statue was the

ABOVE: *The Sphinx, with its lion's body and human face, provides an unexpected naturalistic contrast to the geometric shapes of the pyramids.*

RIGHT: *Excavation of the Sphinx by Ernst Koerner, 1883. The figure was buried for most of its life in the sand. and probably lost its nose 600 years ago. Between 1816 and 1817, the Genoese merchant, Caviglia tried to clear away the sand but he only managed to dig a trench down the chest of the statue and along the length of the forepaws. Auguste Mariette, the founder of the Egyptian Antiquities Service, also attempted to excavate the Sphinx, but gave up in frustration. Between 1925 and 1936, French engineer Emile Baraize excavated the Sphinx on behalf of the Antiquities Service, and apparently for the first time since antiquity, the great beast once again became exposed to the elements.*

The face of the Great Sphinx is believed to be that of Khafre—a fact reinforced by the causeway that goes west-northwest to Khafre's Pyramid. The causeway runs above and along the south wall of the Sphinx enclosure. A mortuary temple stands east of the pyramid on the upper plateau behind the Sphinx.

The Sphinx is the oldest and longest stone sculpture from the Old Kingdom.

largest ever produced in ancient Egypt and remained so for more than 1,000 years until the reigns of Amenhotep III (c.1411–1375 B.C.) and Rameses II (1304–1237 B.C.). Some commentators believe that the Sphinx's face is that of Khafre but others disagree, arguing that it is no more than just a representation of a man's face.

The Sphinx, which may once have been rendered and painted, faces eastward and the head reaches a height of around 66 feet (20m). From tip to tail it is some 240 feet (73m) long and its face is around 14 feet (4m) across at its widest point. Archaeologists believe that the men who built the Sphinx first gouged out a huge U-shaped trench and then carved the interior bed rock into what we see today. The rock that was removed was shaped and used in the construction of a Sphinx Temple. The remains of the Sphinx are in varying degrees of repair in part due to the underlying geology. The body is made of a less hard-wearing stone and has suffered more from erosion that the head, which is a more durable stone. However, the head has lost both its nose and beard.

There has been considerable debate over the precise nature of the Sphinx's religious and ceremonial roles. Some have suggested that its lion shape reflects the importance of such creatures in the mythology of ancient Egypt and that it was positioned to guard the entrances to the Underworld that lay to the east and west.

Some have suggested that there was a belief that when a king died he became the sun-god Atum and that the Sphinx's face is that of Khafre transformed into Atum. Others argue that the Sphinx's role was simply that of a tomb guardian and it is this view of the Sphinx as a protector of the dead that is considered the most likely explanation of its function.

LEFT: *Carved out of a natural limestone outcrop, the Sphinx is 65ft (19.8m) high and 240ft (73.2m) long. During the eighteenth dynasty, it was called "Horus of the Horizon" and "Horus of the Necropolis." The sand has been its savior, since being built of soft sandstone, it would have disappeared long ago had it not been buried for much of its existence. The rectangular structure known as the Sphinx Temple lies directly east of the statue. Adjacent and south of the Sphinx Temple lies a structure known as the Khafre Valley Temple.*

RIGHT: *The Sphinx and Khafre's Pyramid. The main body sits along an east-west axis facing east. An enclosure of open floor surrounds the monument, narrowing somewhat in the western back end. There is an unfinished shelf along the western back wall slightly elevated from the rest of the enclosure floor. Large and small blocks of harder limestone, applied at different times in the past, form a protective covering or facing over the lower parts of the monument.*

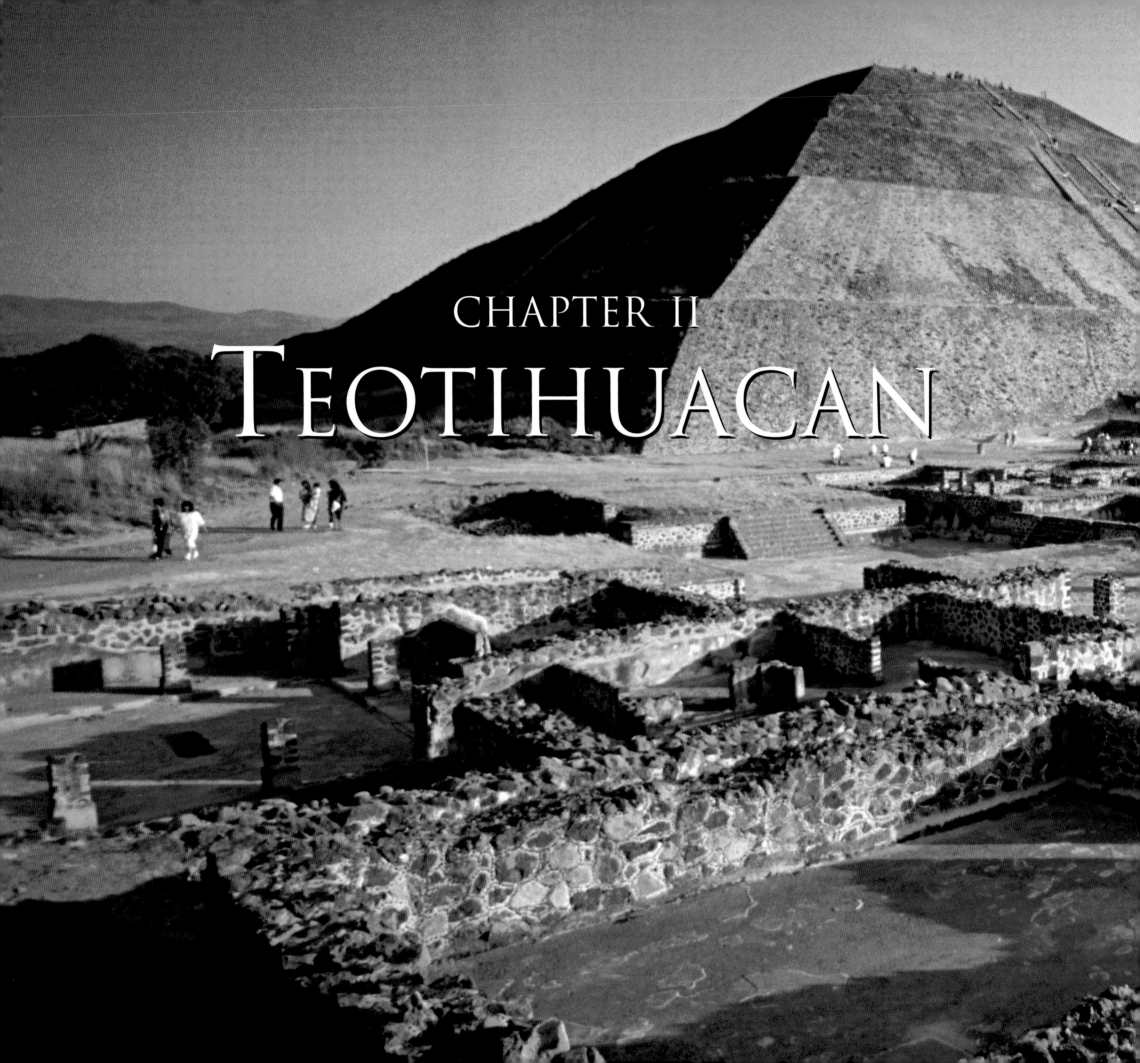

CHAPTER II
TEOTIHUACAN

TEOTIHUACAN

THE LARGEST CITY IN THE ANCIENT AMERICAS

ABOVE: *Locator map–Teotihuacan in Mexico.*

PREVIOUS PAGE: *Evening light at Teotihuacan, looking over toward the Pyramid of the Sun. Teotihuacan, the City of the Gods, grew up around the central axis of the Avenue of the Dead. It contains the oldest and largest pyramids in the New World.*

RIGHT: *View from the top of the Pyramid of the Moon, looking out over the Plaza of the Moon and down the Avenue of the Dead toward the Pyramid of the Sun.*

The ancient city of Teotihuacan in what is now Mexico is by any standards an impressive place. Situated in the Valley of Mexico some 31 miles (50km) northeast of central Mexico City, it is regarded as the earliest known city in the Americas and its imposing remains suggest the great power wielded by an early pre-Columbian civilization.

The name now given to the city was actually not coined by the original inhabitants but by the later Aztecs, who believed that the current cycle of time began at Teotihuacan, which actually means "Place of the Gods." The chief problem confronting today's archaeologists is that no one is quiet sure which people originally occupied the site. Some have pointed to the Olmeca-Xicalanca, or a people who spoke the Mixtec language, or a tribe known as the Totonac. The most likely suggestion is that they founders pre-dated the Toltecs and Aztecs and spoke either Nahuatl or Mixtec.

TEOTIHUACAN'S EARLY HISTORY

Although the builders of the city remain something of a mystery, it is known that Teotihuacan was probably first settled in what is known as the Late Formative Period between 600 and 200 B.C. and underwent a time of major expansion in the Terminal Formative Period between 200 B.C.–A.D. 200. It was during this period that the remains we see today and the city's grid pattern were laid out. Teotihuacan's total population is estimated to have been some 125,000–200,000 people, making it probably the sixth biggest urban center in the world when the city was at its peak. The scale of the city has gradually been revealed by archaeologists during the last four decades or so. The Teotihuacan Mapping Project published a map in 1973 that showed the extent of the city between roughly 100 B.C. and A.D. 750. Taken together, the ceremonial, religious, and residential areas covered some eight square miles (20sq km). The ordinary folk lived in something like 2,000 large rectangular building complexes known as apartment compounds that probably housed family groups of some 60 to 100 people of all ages. Some of these living quarters have been reconstructed for the benefit of visitors.

Teotihuacan's power reached its zenith during the Classic Period in around 400 A.D. when it probably had influence over a vast swathe of territory that took in the southern two-thirds of what is now Mexico, all of Guatamala and Belize, as well as parts of Honduras and El Salvador. It appears unlikely that this was an empire carved out and occupied by the original founders of Teotihuacan using violence but it is thought that these various lands simply paid tribute to honor the city's influence. There is no doubting Teotihuacan's power as its architectural styles, ceramics, and obsidian (a volcanic glass) tools have been uncovered all across the areas previously mentioned.

THE CEREMONIAL HEART OF THE CITY

The ceremonial heart of the city covers approximately 5 square miles (12.9sq km) and most of Teotihuacan's major buildings lie around a 1.2-mile (2km) north-south roadway known today as the *Calzada de los Muertos* (Avenue of the Dead). It gained its title from the Aztecs, who thought that ancient rulers were buried along its length. Archaeologists think that the alignment of the Avenue of the Dead, which is 13 degrees to the east of north, was of astronomical significance to the city's inhabitants. The avenue essentially connects two of the city's most important sites, the *Piramide de la Luna* (Pyramid of the Moon), which lies to the north and the *Templo de Quetzalcoatl* (Temple of Quetzalcoatl), which is at its southern end.

Elsewhere along its length are the palaces of the city rulers and most influential citizens as well as more if smaller stepped pyramids and some government buildings. Teotihuacan's most important ceremonial structure, the *Piramide del Sol* (Pyramid of the Sun) was built to the east of the Avenue of the Dead. Based on this evidence, archaeologists believe that the original inhabitants built their city around the four cardinal points of the compass and that there was once an

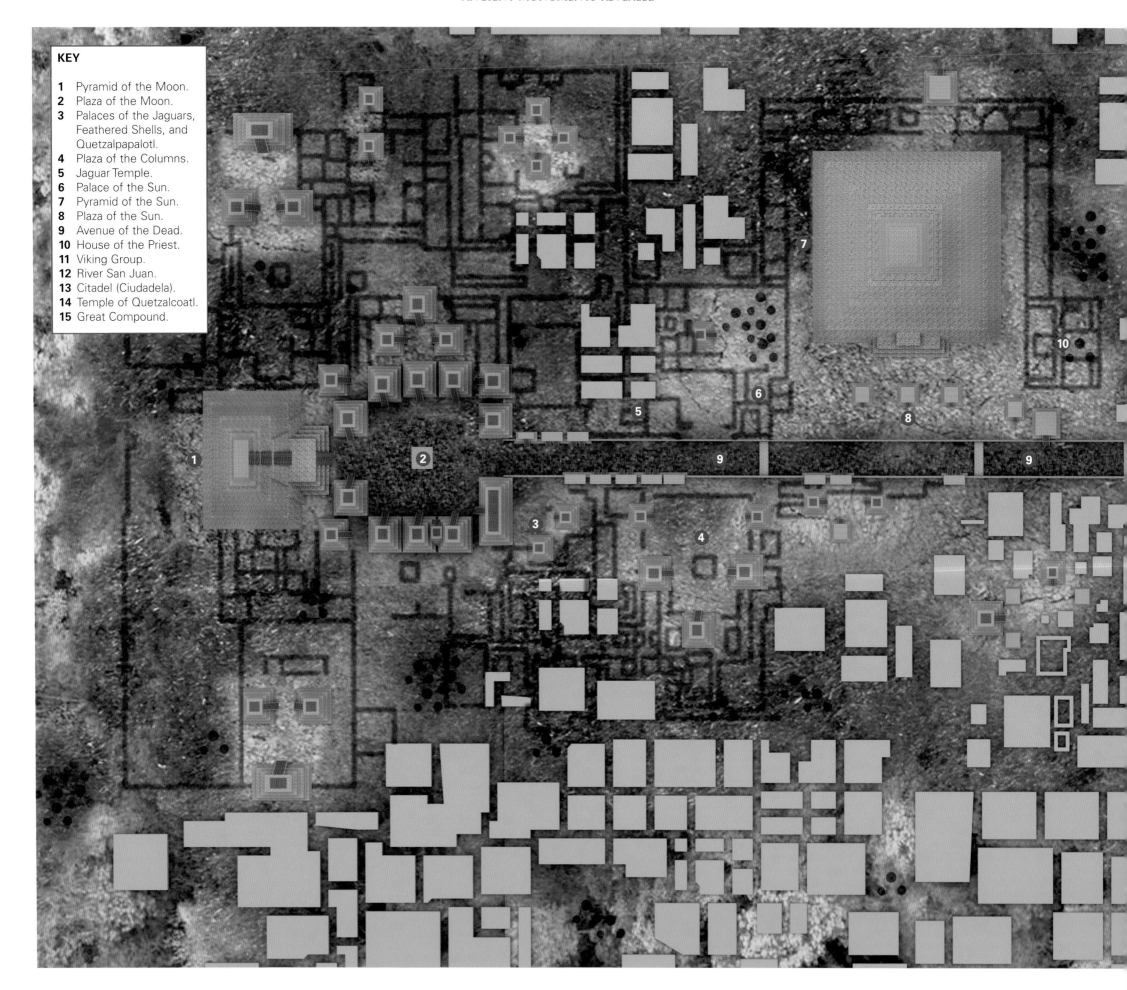

KEY

1 Pyramid of the Moon.
2 Plaza of the Moon.
3 Palaces of the Jaguars, Feathered Shells, and Quetzalpapalotl.
4 Plaza of the Columns.
5 Jaguar Temple.
6 Palace of the Sun.
7 Pyramid of the Sun.
8 Plaza of the Sun.
9 Avenue of the Dead.
10 House of the Priest.
11 Viking Group.
12 River San Juan.
13 Citadel (Ciudadela).
14 Temple of Quetzalcoatl.
15 Great Compound.

east-to-west roadway of equal significance to the Avenue of the Dead. The *Ciudadela* (Citadel) was built at the southern end of the Avenue of the Dead and it was given its current name by the Spanish conquistadores who mistakenly thought that it resembled a barracks for troops. In reality it was used as a home for the city's leading administrators and high priests. The large enclosed structure consisted of four wide walls each 1,300 feet (390m) long that are topped by a number of pyramids. The large courtyard of the Ciudadela is dominated by another pyramid, the Temple of Quetzalcoatl, the feathered serpent. The structure lies in the eastern part of the square and is flanked by ruined rooms and patio areas that were probably the domain of Teotihuacan's numerous administrators.

During excavations of the site, archaeologists discovered that the temple had been built over an even earlier structure dating from around A.D. 250–300. Four steps of the structure's facade remain in situ (originally there were seven) and they are covered with a series of remarkable carvings. Examples of these include a feathered serpent with sharp fangs that has its head rising out of a necklace made up of 11 petals. There is another two-fanged creature with four eyes that has been variously identified as Tlaloc, the rain god, or as the fire serpent that carried the sun on its daily journey across the sky. All of these carvings would have once been painted and some still have spots of the red paint that was used by the original artists. This came from the body fluids of tiny bugs that the locals had crushed.

The stepped, steep-sided Pyramid of the Sun lies due north of the Ciudadela across the San Juan River that separates the southern third of the site from the rest. This remarkable feat of engineering was begun in the late Pre-Classical Period, in

RIGHT: *Closeup of pyramids surrounding the Plaza of the Moon in front of the Pyramid of the Moon. The huge Pyramid of the Sun is in the background.*

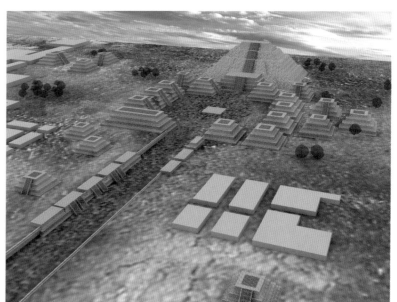

THIS PAGE: *Much of Teotihuacan has still to be excavated but is clear that the city was built on a grid plan with the two-mile long Avenue of the Dead as the central axis. Around this were built a number of pyramids, palaces, temples, and other buildings all in the same unique architectural style known as "talud-tablero" in which the sloping walls are covered with decorative panels. At the southern end of the Avenue of the Dead is a gigantic complex known as the Ciudadela (Citadel). This includes the Temple of Quetzalcoatl and the main plaza which could easily contain a crowd of over 60,000 people.*

RIGHT: *This image shows the main temples along Teotihuacan's Avenue of the Dead. The blue line indicates the course of the San Juan River through the city. It was used as the main sewer by Teotihuacan's inhabitants.*

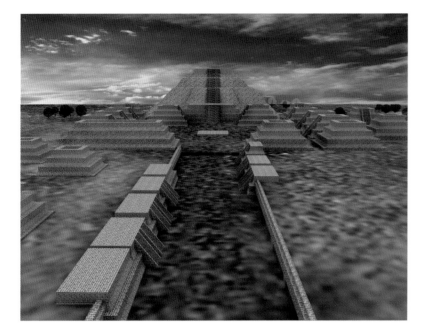

THIS PAGE: *At its peak in 600 A.D. Teotihuacan had around 100,000 inhabitants who lived within a well defined social structure. Their highly sophisticated society was based on agriculture, trade, and obsidian mining and revolved around a 260-day sacred calendar. They counted and calculated using a bar and dot number system and had knowledge of writing and books. The majority of the site remains covered by jungle—even though conventional archaeologists have been working here for over a century—but the ceremonial civic center area alone covers over two square miles. It is bisected by the Avenue of the Dead. This runs for almost two miles but is broken up at intervals along its length by walled courtyards near important structures. Some scholars think that the Aztecs possibly lined this route with their mummified ancestors and hence the name of the avenue.*

around A.D. 100, and was completed some 50 years later. It is the world's second largest such structure behind that at Cholula in Puebla to the south of Mexico City and is comparable in size to that of the Great Pyramid of Khufu at Giza in Egypt. Its four sides are not quite square as it measures some 728 feet (222m) by 738 feet (225m); its current height is around 197 feet (60m)—the summit is reached by 248 steps—and archaeologists estimate that it was built from a staggering three million tons of brick, stone, and rubble. It is faced with stone that was originally painted bright red and the other materials were used in the interior, and there is some evidence to indicate it was built over an earlier pyramid of not dissimilar size.

It was the Aztecs who believed that the pyramid was built to honor the sun god and their view was confirmed during excavations carried out in 1971. Archaeologists uncovered a 328 foot (100m) tunnel on its west side that runs down to a natural cave directly beneath the center of the pyramid. They have suggested that the sun god was originally worshipped in the cave on the basis of religious artifacts uncovered there and that the pyramid—indeed, all of Teotihuacan—grew up because of this natural feature's importance to the city's original inhabitants.

The next building of significance lies between the Pyramid of the Sun and the Pyramid of the Moon on the western side of the Avenue of the Dead to the southwest corner of the Plaza de la Luna (Square of the Moon). It has been variously suggested that the Palacio de Quetzalpapalotl (Palace of the Quetzal Butterfly) was either a royal residence or home to a high-ranking priest. Entrance to the structure is by way of a flight of steps that leads to a roofed portico that houses carvings and glyphs of birds (symbolic figures carved or incised in relief). Images of the plumed butterfly that gave the building its name are carved into the columns that support the roof.

The next sites of interest lie behind and below the Palace of Quetzalpapalotl.

ABOVE: *The Pyramid of the Sun is the third largest pyramid in the world and was built in the first century* A.D. *It has a volume of 2.5 million tons of stone and earth and is in* reality *a succession of pyramids built one on top of the other over time. On May 19 and July 25 the sun in the morning directly faces the east face; at noon it is directly overhead,* *and then faces the west face full on as it sets. There is a good museum to the south of the pyramid.*

RIGHT: *During Teotihuacan's heyday most of the city was plastered and the pyramids were painted bright red.*

ABOVE: *The Temple of Quetzalcoatl—the Plumed Serpent—is at the south end of the Avenue of the Dead.*

The first is the *Palacio de los Jaguares* (Palace of the Jaguars) is reached through a short entrance maze. It takes its name from the murals that adorn some of the lower walls of the chambers that surround the patio. These depict the jaguar god adorned with a feathered headdress and blowing a conch while apparently praying to Tlaloc, the god of rain. The site has been extensively restored but some of the original frescoes showing birds, corn and water picked out in green, red, white and yellow remain visible elsewhere.

Entrance to the next major structure, The *Templo de los Caracoles Emplumados* (Temple of the Plumed Conch Shells), is by way of the Palace of the Jaguars. This below-ground building dates from either the second or third century A.D. and has several noteworthy carvings. The facade is covered in the shells that give the temple its name and the conches, which were probably used as musical instruments, are depicted with feathers and flowers with four petals. The base below the facade is highly coloured and shows birds with water pouring out of their beaks, all brightly painted in blue, green, red and yellow.

A second four-sided pyramid, the Pyramid of the Moon, is at the northern terminal of the Avenue of the Dead. Although not actually as tall as the Pyramid of the Sun to the south, it appears a similar height because it is built on slightly higher ground. Archaeologists believe that it was constructed slightly later than the Pyramid of the Sun, in around 300 A.D., and found a sculpture of the water goddess, Chalchlutilcue while carrying out excavations. The Plaza of the Moon lies directly in front of the pyramid and consists of 12 raised temple platforms. Experts have suggested that these together with the pyramid—that is 13 structures in all—were of astronomical importance to the city's population as the number played a major role in the counting of days in the pre-Columbian ritual calendar. The square also contains an altar at its center, which is thought to have been for dancing during religious ceremonies.

Some of the best preserved frescoes can be found at the *Palacio de Tepantitla* (Palace of Tepantitla), which stands some 545 feet (500m) to the southeast of the Pyramid of the Moon. The building was home to a high priest and it contains what

ABOVE: *The Pyramid of Quetzalcoatl boasts exquisitely rendered heads of the serpent god. Quetzalcoatl.*

RIGHT: *Quetzalcoatl was an important god in Mesoamerican mythology whose name was used by many Toltec monarchs. The word comes from the Nahuatl language—the most important Native American language best known for its use by the Aztecs, but now thought to have been used in earlier Teotihuacan periods. The cult of the snake is very old in Mesoamerica—but in Teotihuacan the snake became Quetzalcoatl, the plumed serpent. The god became more and more important as time went on, gaining other attributes and associations—such as with the wind god, the morning star (Venus), rain, and in the end became wrapped up in creation myths. In one story Quetzalcoatl was sent into exile by sea, on a raft of snakes. Some believe that Montezuma, the Aztec king, thought that Cortes and the Conquistadores were Quetzalcoatl returning from exile— although this is debated by some historians.*

Bird's eye view of the Temple of the Moon. The south-facing Pyramid of the Moon is at the northern end of the Avenue of the Dead. The best views of the city are from the top of this temple. The Pyramid of the Moon was built a few years after the taller Pyramid of the Sun (center left), although it appears to be the same size because it was built on slightly higher ground.

many consider to be Teotihuacan's most renowned frescoes. These lie either side of a doorway in a covered area in the northeast corner of the structure. They depict Tlaloc, the god of rain, being attended by priests. Below these and to the right of the door is an impressive piece of art that reveals the world in which he lived, a veritable Garden of Eden filled with fish swimming in a mountain stream, people and various animals. To the left of the doorway is another mural, one with people playing a type of ball game; and elsewhere in the building visitors will come across what are thought to be murals of priests wearing feather head-dresses.

There is another important site of interest that is sometimes overlooked because it lies outside the main complex of buildings and outside the road that

encircles them. To the northwest of the main entrance gate in the southwest corner of the city, are a number of quite substantial palaces. Their many murals, many of which have survived pretty much intact or have been expertly restored, were first discovered in the 1940s. Perhaps the finest collect of murals lies in the *Palacio de Tetitla* (Palace of Tetitla), where around 120 walls have been adorned with artwork. The familiar rosta of subjects can be seen on them, including Tlaloc, birds of prey, jaguars, and serpents.

Further murals, both originals and restorations, can be found in the *Palacio de Atetelco* (Palace of Atetelco), which stands around 365 feet (400m) to the west of the Palace of Tetitla. The best murals are situated in what is known as the *Patio Blanco* (White Patio) and these consist of processions of coyotes and jaguars in

BELOW: *The steep sides of the Pyramid of the Sun have been carefully restored.*

ABOVE AND RIGHT: *Quetzalcoatl's head is a feature in Teotihuacan. The Aztecs were the cultural heirs of the Toltecs and so it isn't surprising that they took over and expanded* *Quetzalcoatl's role. Indeed, the plumed serpent symbol can be found among many American Indian peoples from the Hopi in the north to the Andes. in the south.*

LEFT: *Architectural sculpture with serpent heads and masks on the Temple of Quetzalcoatl.*

various shades of red. Two further buildings of interest stand to the northeast of the Palace de Atetelco. These are a pair of large walled compounds with many rooms and are known as Yayahuala and Zacuala. They were both home to large family groups.

TEOTIHUACAN'S LATER HISTORY

None one is quite sure what caused the enfeeblement of the one great city that took place in the eighth century A.D. Various long-standing economic, social, and political reasons have been put forward to explain its demise. Did it suffer a catastrophic loss of its inhabitants due to sickness or plague? It seems certain that insanitary conditions in the past had led to high rates of mortality and that the city's population was only maintained by a steady flow of immigrants. Perhaps this replacement system broke down. Others have suggested that the over-exploitation of natural resources , especially wood, hastened its end. It is known that a great fire in around 750 A.D. destroyed much of the ceremonial and administrative heart of the city. The population appears to have declined rapidly following this catastrophe and there were few still in residence by 850 A.D.

Teotihuacan was never entirely abandoned but it never regained either its power or its prestige. However, its influence did not disappear entirely. Many of the gods worshipped in the city, such as Quetzalcoatl and Tlaloc, were adopted by the later Aztecs when they rose to prominence in the fourteenth–fifteenth centuries and whose royalty made regular pilgrimages to the site. Teotihuacan

became of academic interest only in the comparatively recent past. Modern archaeology at the site really got underway in 1906 under the orders of an authoritarian ruler, General Porifirio Diaz, who wanted to show the world Mexico's cultural heritage and have the site ready for public display by 1910, to celebrate the hundredth anniversary of the first major revolution against the Spanish.

Teotihuacan has two museums. The first, the *Museo del Sitio* (Site Museum), can be found a little to the south of the Pyramid of the Sun and was built to imitate the shapes and colors used by the city's original inhabitants. It has displays with commentaries in both English and Spanish that show the technologies used by the city's builders, discusses the ways in which Teotihuacan's economy and society were organized and the inhabitants' religious practices. Visitors can also walk over a plexiglass floor below which lies a large-scale model depicting how the city looked at the height of its power. It should be noted that the works of art and the like on display are copies and not the originals, which are housed in the *Museo Nacional de Antropologia* (National Museum of Anthropology) in Mexico City. The site museum is surround by various other amenities, including a botanical garden, a picnic area, toilets and a bookstore.

A second museum well worth a visit is the Museo de la Pintura Mural Teotihuacana (Museum of Teotihuacan's Painted Murals), which was built a little to the north of Gate 2 on the road that rings the city. It has displays of actual murals recovered from the city and also recreations of many that can still be found in situ. The museum is open from 10am to 6pm daily and admission is free with an entrance ticket. The main site is open from 7 am to 6 pm every day and it has five main entrances, although that at the southwest corner is the most used as it is where the buses to and from Mexico City arrive and depart.

ABOVE: *Carved mask of Quetzalcoatl.
Quetzalcoatl was the sacred plumed serpent
and preeminent deity whose image is found
all around the city. His temple at Teotihuacan
is decorated with butterflies.*

RIGHT: *One of a number of carved stone
serpent heads on the side of the Temple of
Quetzalcoatl.*

CHAPTER III
THE ACROPOLIS

THE ACROPOLIS

THE JEWEL OF THE CLASSICAL GREEK WORLD

ABOVE: *Locator map–The Acropolis is in Athens, Greece.*

PREVIOUS PAGE: *The Acropolis at night.*

The Acropolis (high point of the city) is the enduring jewel of the Classical Greek world and was the heart of the ancient Athenian city-state, acting as its symbolic and religious center. Indeed, it was the very spot where mythology tells us that Athens was born.

The actual site is a flat-topped rectangular limestone outcrop some 512 feet (150m) above sea level. It is visible for miles around across the Plains of Attica and was deliberately chosen to impress and awe any visitor to the city. It seems likely that the Acropolis was first occupied during the Neolithic period (late Stone Age) between roughly 9000 and 4000 B.C., although the evidence is scant. There is better evidence for more recent occupation of the site. Archaeologists have uncovered the remains of a 16-foot (5m) thick defensive wall below the Temple of Athena Nike that predates the Classical Greek era and once completely encircled the Acropolis. It seems that this relates to the Mycenaean Bronze Age civilization that began to dominate mainland Greece from around 1500 B.C., and the Acropolis then was used as both palace and temple. The cult of Athena, the goddess of wisdom who gave the city its name, probably emerged during the eleventh century B.C., but the first temples dedicated to her on the Acropolis did not actually appear until about 650 B.C., a time when the city was run by the *Aristoi*, a clique of landowners.

Their preferred form of government was known as aristocracy, meaning the rule of the best—in reality this really meant just the wealthy.

THE ORIGINS OF THE CLASSICAL ACROPOLIS

The "true" Acropolis began to take shape in 507 B.C., when the ruling elite was overthrown by a faction headed by Cleisthenes and the city-state began to experiment with a new form of government—democracy or rule of the people. In 490 B.C. work began to construct a new temple on the summit of the Acropolis but it took the outbreak of war with Persia nine years later to add impetus to the construction program. Athens joined with other Greek city-states to form a mutual defence organization known as the Delian League. Victory and the independence of the Greek city-states was secured with the naval victory at the Battle of Salamis off Cyprus in 450 B.C. and the signing of the Peace of Callias two years later. After some 30 years of warfare, the pre-eminence of Persia in the ancient world was ended, Greek supremacy was assured and Athens, as the head of the league, was left the most powerful city-state.

Although Athens had been fighting a costly war during this period, it was actually awash with money chiefly because of one man, Pericles (c. 490-429 B.C.). A leading democrat and de facto head of

state from 461 B.C., he was largely responsible for maintaining the confederation of city-states but was also guilty of expropriating taxes paid by them to Athens to fund the ongoing war with Persia. Some of the money was actually used to finance an extensive program of building work on the Acropolis using the greatest architects and artists in Greece. Pericles continued the expropriations long after the end of the Graeco-Persian War and work on the so-called Periclean project proceeded even after he was overthrown in 430 B.C. Pericles' legacy can be seen in several of the finest building on the Acropolis, including the Erechtheion, the Propylaea, the Temple of Athena Nike, and of course, the majestic Parthenon.

The entrance to the Acropolis lies in the southwest corner of the rocky outcrop. The Classical Greek ramp that originally led up to the site has long gone but modern visitors pass by the ruins of the Roman-built Buele Gate, which is named after the French archaeologist who excavated it, and then move through the imposing gateway known as the Propylaea, which had columns of Penteli marble. It was the brainchild of the architect and engineer Mnesikles and construction began in 437 B.C. The Propylaea was never completed as the work ceased some five years later largely due to the outbreak of the Second Peloponnesian War (432–404 B.C.). Nevertheless, the remains

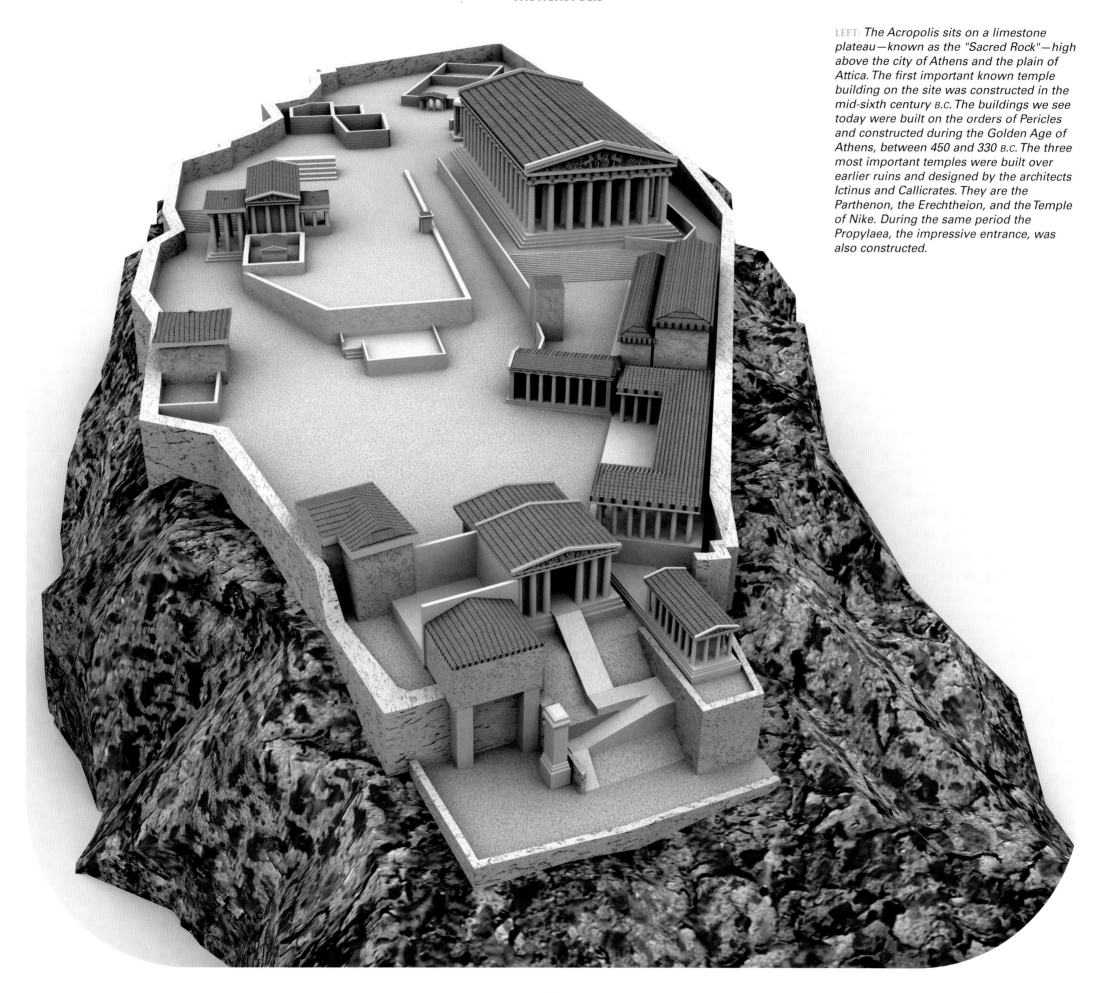

LEFT: *The Acropolis sits on a limestone plateau—known as the "Sacred Rock"—high above the city of Athens and the plain of Attica. The first important known temple building on the site was constructed in the mid-sixth century B.C. The buildings we see today were built on the orders of Pericles and constructed during the Golden Age of Athens, between 450 and 330 B.C. The three most important temples were built over earlier ruins and designed by the architects Ictinus and Callicrates. They are the Parthenon, the Erechtheion, and the Temple of Nike. During the same period the Propylaea, the impressive entrance, was also constructed.*

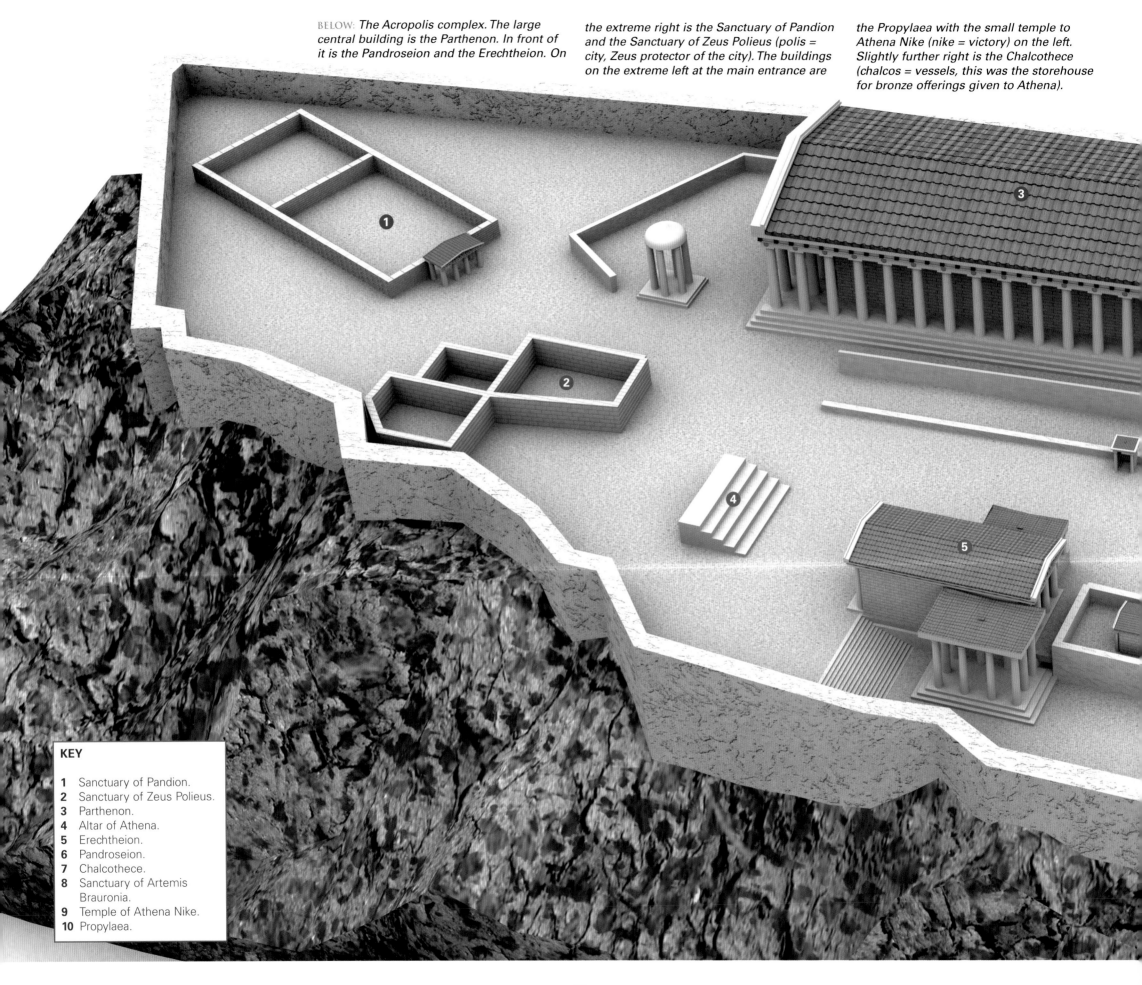

BELOW: The Acropolis complex. The large central building is the Parthenon. In front of it is the Pandroseion and the Erechtheion. On the extreme right is the Sanctuary of Pandion and the Sanctuary of Zeus Polieus (polis = city, Zeus protector of the city). The buildings on the extreme left at the main entrance are the Propylaea with the small temple to Athena Nike (nike = victory) on the left. Slightly further right is the Chalcothece (chalcos = vessels, this was the storehouse for bronze offerings given to Athena).

KEY

1 Sanctuary of Pandion.
2 Sanctuary of Zeus Polieus.
3 Parthenon.
4 Altar of Athena.
5 Erechtheion.
6 Pandroseion.
7 Chalcothece.
8 Sanctuary of Artemis Brauronia.
9 Temple of Athena Nike.
10 Propylaea.

more than hint at its beauty. Mnesikles successfully combined Doric and Ionic styles of architecture to outstanding effect. The gateway was also beautifully decorated. Its north wing was known as the Pinakothiki (art gallery) and it contained numerous reclining seats from where visitors could enjoy scenes from the writings of Homer (fl. eighth century B.C.).

The first building of note, the Temple of Athena Nike, stands on the cliff edge to the right rear of the Propylaea and rises above the main entrance to the Acropolis. Although tiny in comparison to other temples dating from the Classical Greek age, it is generally considered to be of outstanding architectural merit, outshining all others. It was built during a temporary lull in the fighting during the Second Peloponnesian War brought about by the signing of the Treaty of Nicias in 421 B.C. The treaty was supposed to bring peace between Athens and a collection of rival city-states headed by Sparta for 50 years but it actually last just five and hostilities recommenced in 415 B.C. However, the respite did allow the Athenians to build the temple. It is ringed by eight Ionic columns and once housed a statue of Nike, the winged goddess of victory. When war broke out again, the Athenians feared that the goddess would fly away and that their city would fall to the Spartans and their allies, so they clipped the statue's wings.

The temple that visitors see today is, in fact, not the real thing but a copy of the original, which was demolished by the occupying Ottoman Turks in 1686 to make way for artillery emplacements. It was reconstructed in the 1830 and underwent repair between 1935 and 1940. Much of the work done at these times was inaccurate to a greater or lesser degree and in 2000 the Greek authorities orchestrated a major program of works to correct these earlier faults. Pieces of the original temple, chiefly friezes of Greeks battling Persians and representations of various gods, are located in the on-site Acropolis Museum.

THE GLORY OF THE PARTHENON
The Parthenon—or more correctly the Temple of Athena Parthenos (Athena the virgin goddess)—is the centrepiece of the Acropolis and has dominated the Athens' skyline ever since its construction. It was the brainchild of two of Classical Greece's

BELOW: *Bird's eye view of the Acropolis showing the layout of the complex.*

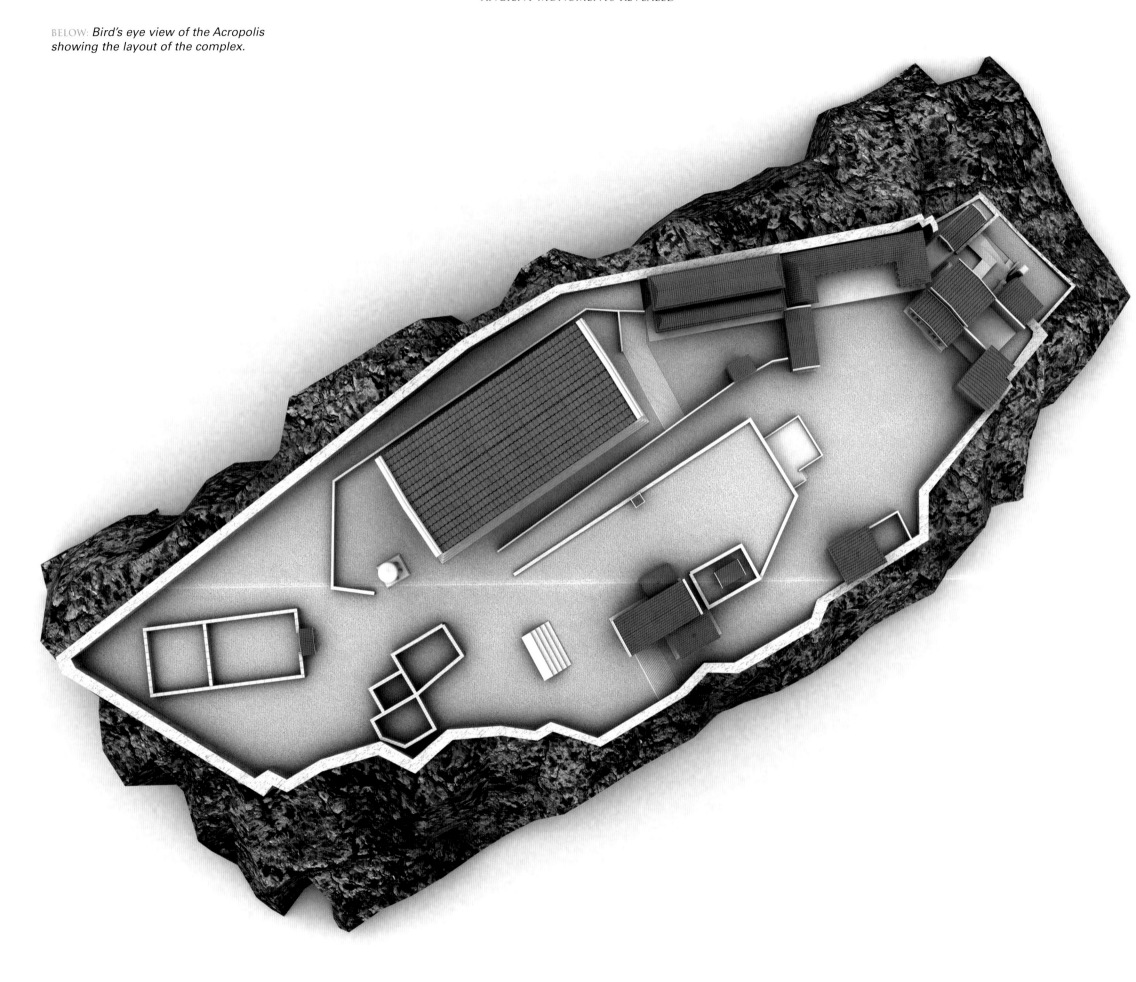

BELOW: *The Propylaea (the grand entrance) was constructed between 437 and 432 B.C. and finished just before the outbreak of the Peloponnesian Wars. The first temple on the right is to Athena Nike and was built to commemorate the Athenians' victory over the Persians.*

greatest sculptor-architects, Ictinus and Phidias, and the building work commenced in 447 B.C. Despite this being an immense undertaking, the work was completed with amazing speed, ending in 438 B.C. The result of this frenzied activity was a temple of exquisite beauty. The Parthenon is perfectly proportioned and reflects the Athenian obsession with geometrical symmetry, in this case everything was built in the ratio of four to nine, a variation of the so-called Golden Mean. This is most evident in the structure's columns. These actually bulge and lean a few degrees inward to counteract the optical illusion that straight lines viewed at a distance appear to bend.

The temple was once richly decorated. Intricate and lively friezes along the axes depicted the Greek gods or the heroes of antiquity, reflecting Athens' rise to pre-eminence among the Greek city-states. However, few of the sculpted panels remain in place. Due to a still-controversial removal program in the nineteenth century (see below) around two-thirds of them were hacked from the Parthenon. On the north side carvings once hailed the Greek victory over the Trojans and on the south side the Lapith (a people of Thessaly ruled by Lapithes, a son of Zeus) battle Centaurs (another people of Thessaly usually represented in classical mythology as half man-half horse) when an

altercation at a wedding feast turned violent. The east side panels depicted the defeat of the Titans at the hands of the gods of Mount Olympus, while the west side had Athens triumphing over the Amazons, a nation of warrior women living in Cappadocia (Asia Minor).

The crowing glory of this artistic triumph were the Parthenon's east and west pediments (the triangular structures each held up by eight columns). The west one echoed the theme of the nearby Erechtheion (see below) and displayed the battle for Athens between Athena and Poseidon. The east one showed in graphic detail the birth of Athena at the moment when she erupted fully formed from the

RIGHT: *The large walled area to the left of the Parthenon is where the earlier Temple to Athena was situated and behind it is the Pandroseion. Pandrosus was the object of mysterious cult worship and was one of the daughters of Cecrops, the first Athenian king.*

BELOW: *The view from the east with the Sanctuary of Pandion in the foreground.*

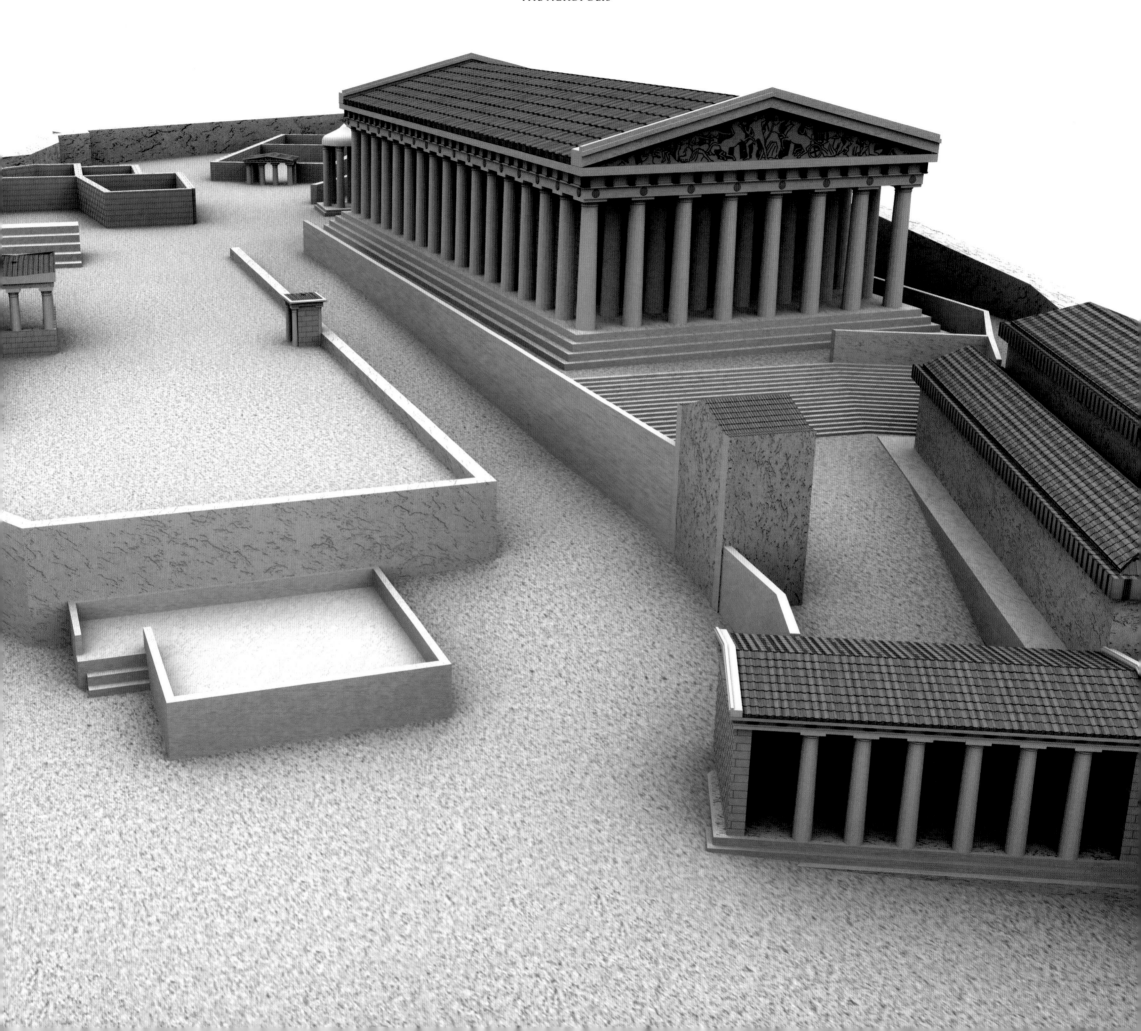

BELOW: *The most important building on the site is the magnificent Parthenon which is dedicated to Athena Parthenos, the patron goddess of Athens. It was designed by the architects Iktinos and Kallikrates and built between 447 and 438 B.C.*

mouth of Zeus, the king and most powerful of all the Greek gods. The interior was also richly decorated and a frieze showed groups of Athenian citizens mingling with the gods. Although long gone, the Parthenon once contained an immense 40-foot (12m) statue of Athena created by Phidias. It was made from gold and ivory (a substance known as chryselephantine) and stood by a pool of water. Nothing of the statue remains but a smaller Roman copy dating from the second century A.D. held by the Greek National Museum gives some idea of the look if not the scale of the original.

THE ACROPOLIS'S OTHER STRUCTURES

A further temple, the Erechtheion, lies to the immediate north of the Parthenon, just across the Avenue of Panathenaic Procession and on the site where it was believed that Athena and Poseidon battled to become the patron of Athens.

Poseidon, the god of the sea, struck his trident into the outcrop to create a spring of water as an offering to the Athenians but Athena trumped this by giving them an olive tree that provided Athens with food, oil, and shelter. She thus became the city's patron.

As the contest actually ended in a truce, the site comprised two temples. The eastern porch with its six Ionic columns once contained an olive-wood statue of Athena, while the western side was given over to Poseidon. The most well-known sculptures found on the Acropolis are part of the Erechtheion. These are the six voluptuous female carvings known as the Caryatids. It has

ABOVE: *The Plain of Attica and the buildings of Athens spread out for miles around the Acropolis which is 412ft (1,109m) high. The plain is surrounded on three sides by mountains and on the fourth by the Aegean Sea. In 1832 Greece won independence from Turkey and in 1834 Athens became the capital of Greece.*

been suggested that they took their name from the women of Caryae, many of whom were enslaved by the Athenians and were renowned for their beauty. Visitors should note that the present-day statues are copies but five of the originals can be seen in the Acropolis Museum and the other is housed at the British Museum in London. The building was finished in 406 B.C., just two years before Athens was defeated by the Spartans in the Second Peloponnesian War.

Other structures on the Acropolis have fared less well than the aforementioned and little of them remains. The temenos (temple enclosure) of Artemis Brauronia lies between the Temple of Athena Nike and the Parthenon. Artemis was the goddess of hunting—commonly represented as a bear—and was worshiped in three festivals (Brauronia) each year. The complex contained a statue of the goddess built by Praxiteles in the fourth century B.C. Other structures included the Chalcotheke, the sanctuary of Zeus Polleus and the circular temple of

ABOVE: *In the foreground at the base of the Acropolis lie the ruins of the Odeum of Herodes. It was built by the Romans around 167 A.D. The long colonnaded walkway is the Stoa of Eumenes which was used as a promenade between the Odeum and the Theater of Dionysus (on the extreme right).*

RIGHT: *Aerial view of the Acropolis from the east. The Roman ruins lie to the south.*

ABOVE: *The imposing mass of the Acropolis was inhabited before 3000 B.C. although the earliest building remains date from the late Bronze Age around 1200 B.C. Most of the buildings we see today date from the sixth century B.C.*

RIGHT: *The Acropolis at night is an impressive sight. The Persians captured and destroyed Athens in 480 B.C. and in the process burned down the buildings on the Acropolis as well as much of the city. Athens was retaken the following year but the emphasis for the next 50 years was on building fortifications instead of temples.*

Augustus that dated from the period after the Roman occupation of Athens.

THE LATER HISTORY OF THE ACROPOLIS

The Acropolis has enjoyed a checkered history, one beginning little more than 20 years after the death of Pericles and at a time when most of the building work had been completed. Athens was defeated in the Second Peloponnesian War and the city, along with the Acropolis, was occupied by the rival city-state of Sparta. This set a precedent for what took place at various times down the centuries. Members of the Byzantine Orthodox Christian faith subsequently took over the Acropolis as a place of worship, renaming the Parthenon as the Church of Ag. Sophia. Next Frankish knights took advantage of the capture of Constantinople, the capital of the Byzantine Empire, by Crusaders during the Fourth Crusade (1202–1204) and occupied the site. They turned the Acropolis into a fortified camp for the benefits of the Dukes de la Roche. The Parthenon eventually regained its religious status and became the Roman Catholic Notre Dame d'Athenes.

ABOVE: *The Erechtheion was built in around 406 B.C. It is most famous for the Caryatids on the southern porch side of the building. The temple is built on the spot where Poseidon and Athena contested who would become patron of the city. Poseidon thrust his trident into the rock and a spring appeared; in return, Athena plunged her spear into the ground and an olive tree grew. Athena was declared the winner and Athens was named after her.*

LEFT: *The huge white marble columns, although slightly damaged, remain remarkably intact considering their vast age and checkered history.*

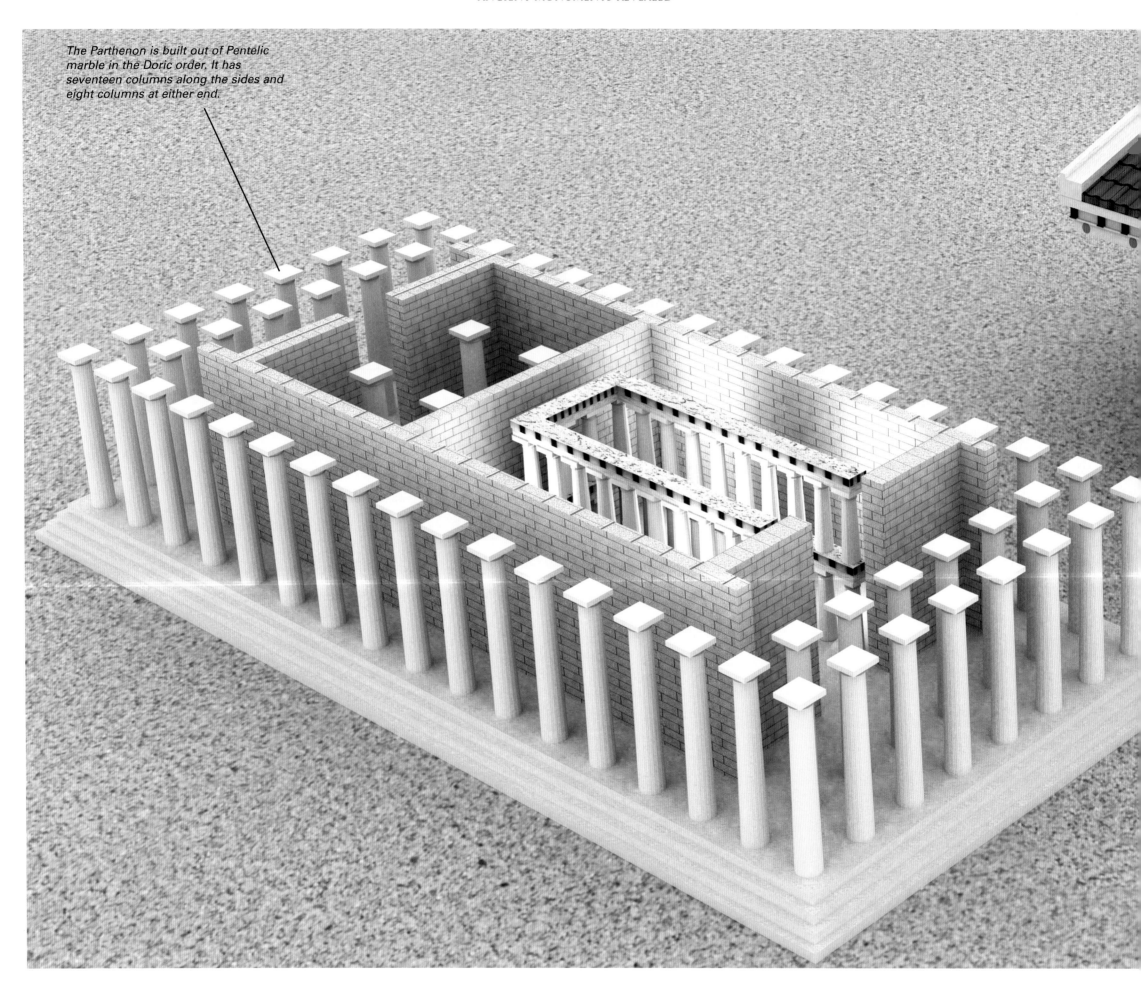

The Parthenon is built out of Pentelic marble in the Doric order. It has seventeen columns along the sides and eight columns at either end.

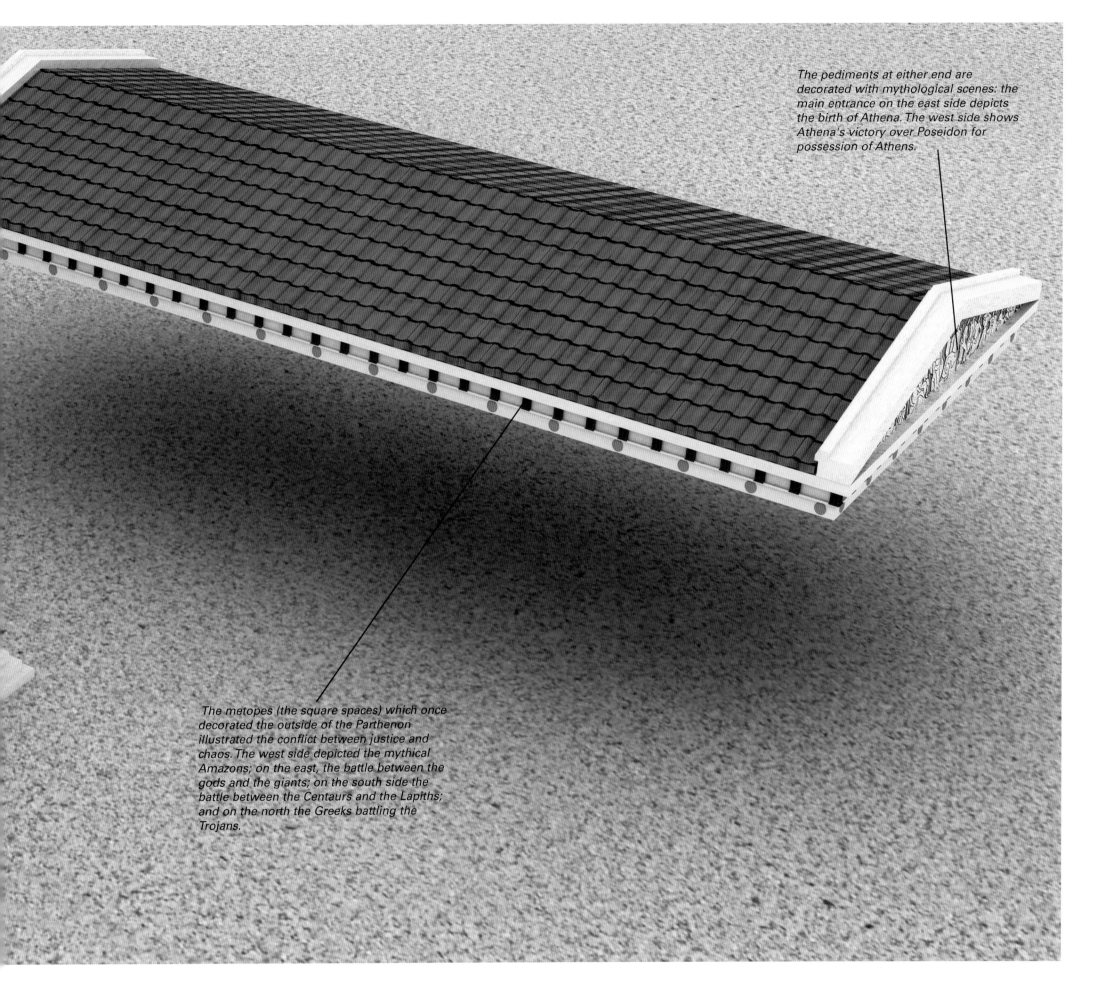

The pediments at either end are decorated with mythological scenes: the main entrance on the east side depicts the birth of Athena. The west side shows Athena's victory over Poseidon for possession of Athens.

The metopes (the square spaces) which once decorated the outside of the Parthenon illustrated the conflict between justice and chaos. The west side depicted the mythical Amazons; on the east, the battle between the gods and the giants; on the south side the battle between the Centaurs and the Lapiths; and on the north the Greeks battling the Trojans.

The Acropolis was next converted into a fortress after the Ottoman Turks took over Greece in 1461—just eight years after they had captured Constantinople and extinguished the last vestiges of the Byzantine Empire. The Parthenon was used as a mosque and the Erechtheion housed the harem of the garrison commander. It was during the Ottoman occupation that the Parthenon suffered major damage thanks to the detonation of gunpowder stored around the site in 1687. The explosion occurred when Venetian shells hit the site during a siege and the explosion blew off the temple's roof. By the 1700s the Parthenon was in an even greater state of disrepair in part thanks to the locals looting its stone for new building work. By the next century the temple faced another threat—that posed by western visitors who wanted a piece of the edifice to add to their own collections of antiquities. The most prolific taker of antiquities from the Parthenon was a Scottish nobleman, Thomas Bruce, the Seventh Earl of Elgin and Twelfth Earl of Kincardine.

RIGHT: *Despite appearances there is not a single right angle or even a straight line in the Parthenon. The entire structure was designed so as to be optically perfect.*

BELOW: *The relief frieze that originally ran around all four sides of the Parthenon shows the Procession of the Panathenaea—the most important ancient Athenian religious festival of the year.*

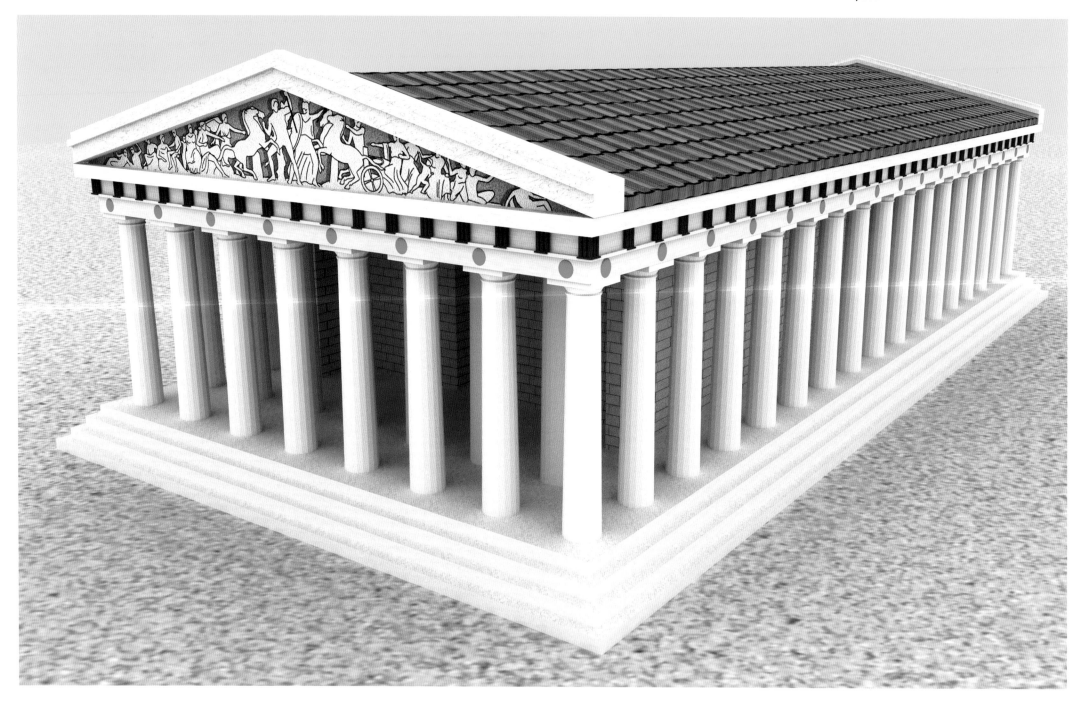

ABOVE AND RIGHT: *The columns throughout the Parthenon were mathematically calculated to be different heights and widths so that the entire building appears absolutely symmetrical. In fact the columns in the center are taller than the ones on either side giving a perfect optical illusion of total symmetry.*

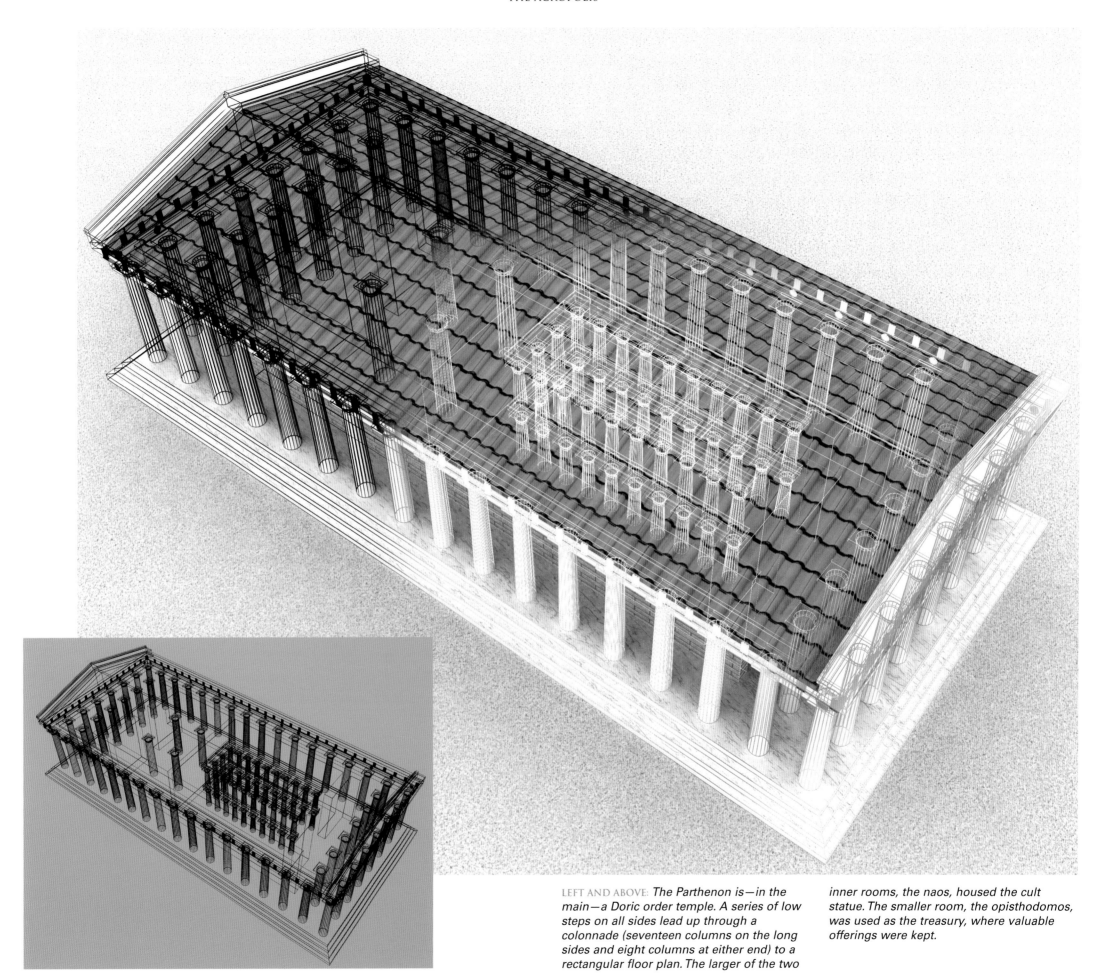

LEFT AND ABOVE: *The Parthenon is—in the main—a Doric order temple. A series of low steps on all sides lead up through a colonnade (seventeen columns on the long sides and eight columns at either end) to a rectangular floor plan. The larger of the two inner rooms, the naos, housed the cult statue. The smaller room, the opisthodomos, was used as the treasury, where valuable offerings were kept.*

ABOVE AND RIGHT: *Originally in the heart of the Parthenon—known as the cella—stood a magnificent chryselephantine cult statue of Athena carved by the great sculptor Phidias,* who was also the supervisor of the entire Acropolis project. She stood within her own columned chamber.

Elgin was an art connoisseur and became interested in the Parthenon while he was the British ambassador to the Ottoman sultan between 1799 and 1803. Arguing that the most complete friezes were likely to deteriorate further because of their ongoing neglect, he subsequently secured the approval of the Ottomans for their removal. These sculptures were sent back to Britain in 1812 and consisted of most of the friezes from the Parthenon's interior, 15 metopes (sculptures between the supporting columns) and numerous others from the building's two triangular pediments. Elgin was much criticized in some quarters for what a number of his contemporaries saw as a wanton act of vandalism but the earl was exonerated of any wrong-doing by a government committee and the treasures were bought for the nation for £5,000 just four years later. The so-called Elgin Marbles are presently on display in the British Museum, despite repeated requests from successive Greek governments that they be returned to the country of origin so that they can be displayed in their correct context.

A few years after Elgin's departure, the Acropolis again came under threat during the Greek War of Independence from the Ottoman Empire. Greek nationalists were besieged in the Acropolis and the complex suffered further damage. Victory was finally won in 1829 and a outsider was brought in to rule the newly independent state. Prince Otto, a Bavarian noble by birth, was also a philhellene, a lover of all things relating to Classical Greece. After his lavish coronation on the Acropolis, he toyed with the idea of building a new palace on its summit but the plan was fortunately abandoned. He opted to removal all traces of post-Classical building on the site and restore it as far as possible to its origin state.

The first major wave of restoration began in 1898 and last for around 40 years. The main effort was the demolition of the final traces of non-Classical structures and the rebuilding of the Temple of Athena Nike. This work of preservation continues to the present day—the Acropolis seems permanently dwarfed by large cranes and swathed in scaffolding—but the Parthenon and other structures remain under threat, and not just from the ravages of time. Today, the major danger is acid rain largely caused by the pollution generated by the cars that clog the overcrowded streets of Athens. It

ABOVE: *Much of the sculptural decoration of the Parthenon is missing and is the subject of great controversy. Lord Elgin bought the marbles from the Turks and in the process* *probably saved them from destruction: the Greeks on the other hand claim that the marbles were stolen and should be returned from the British Museum.*

has become so bad that many items previously left outside for visitors to enjoy are now housed under cover in the on-site museum. Visitors should note that there is an admission charge to the Acropolis which is open between January and March.

ABOVE AND RIGHT: *As well as a Greek temple the Parthenon has at various times been converted into a Byzantine church, a Latin church, and a Muslim mosque. The Parthenon remained in good condition until the seventeenth century when the Turks (who controlled Athens at the time) used the Parthenon as a gunpowder store. Unfortunately, during Admiral Morosini's 1687 siege, a stray Venetian bomb hit the Acropolis destroying much of the building.*

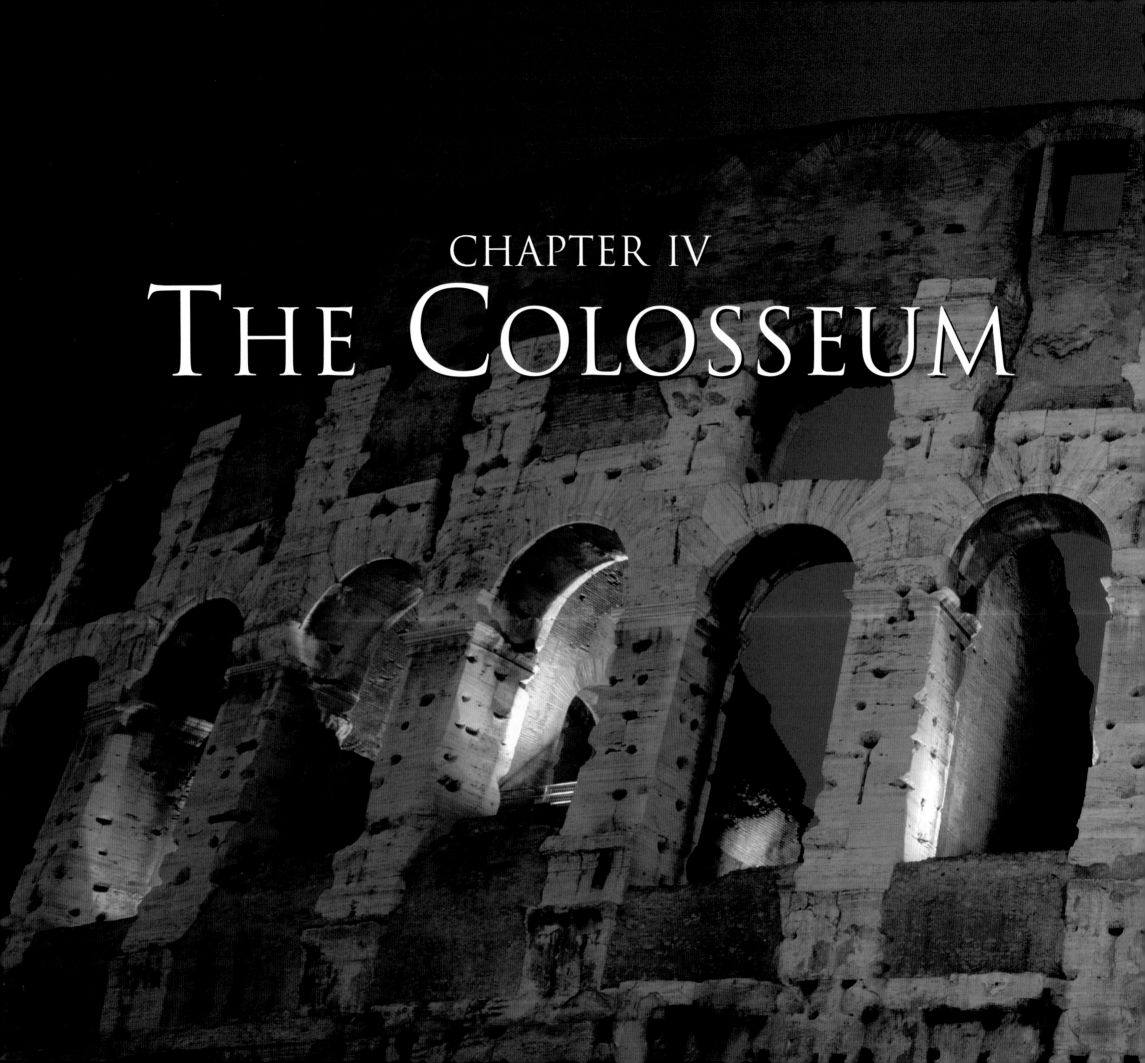

CHAPTER IV
THE COLOSSEUM

THE COLOSSEUM

THE FIRST MASS-ENTERTAINMENT ARENA

ABOVE: *Locator map–The Colosseum, or Coliseum, in Rome, Italy.*

PREVIOUS PAGE: *The Colosseum has stood the test of time and still remains remarkably intact considering its location and age.*

RIGHT: *Model of Ancient Rome showing the Colosseum and the complex of Ludus Magnus.*

Although they are still truly impressive, the ruins of the Colosseum in Rome can only hint at the original architectural splendor of what remains the largest amphitheater ever built. Thanks to the ravages of time, wholesale looting, and general neglect over several centuries, the modern viewer sees only around one-third of the original structure.

The building was commissioned by Titus Flavius Vespasianus (ruled A.D. 69–79), more commonly known as Vespasian and the founder of the Flavian dynasty of Roman emperors. He came to power at a time of dangerous instability in Rome—three emperors of the previous late Claudian dynasty had briefly held the throne between A.D. 68–69 but had done little and two of them, Galba and Vespasian's immediate predecessor, Vitellius, had been assassinated. This instability and uncertainty was damaging the empire and Vespasian needed to reinvigorate the capital, not least to secure his own position. He had to enhance his own prestige, impress senior members of Roman society, and win the approval of the masses.

BUILDING THE COLOSSEUM

The new emperor, who had made his name as a warrior and administrator in Germany, Britain, North Africa, and Palestine, was known for the simplicity of his own lifestyle and, armed with this

moral authority, he was able to impose order on the city's government and finances once he had returned there in A.D. 70. As part of his plan to revitalize Rome, he embarked on a major program of civic works that included the creation of a vast amphitheater, one funded by war booty. The site chosen for the new arena was what had once been a lake in the grounds of the Emperor Nero's former home, the Domus Aurea (Golden House). Work commenced in A.D. 72 and the emerging oval structure was originally simply known as the Flavian amphitheater but became known by its current name either because it stood near a giant (but now long gone) 120-foot (37m) statue of Nero (A.D. 54–68) known as the Colosseum or because of its own immense dimensions. The Colosseum was incomplete when its founder died, but the work was carried on under the rule of the next emperor, Vespasian's son, Titus Flavius Sabinus Vespasianus (A.D. 79–81). It was finally completed during the reign of Titus's brother and possible murderer, Domitian, who reigned between A.D. 81 and A.D. 96.

In its final form the exterior of the Colosseum had a circumference of 1,788 feet (555m), was approximately 620 feet long (189m) and 512 feet (156m) wide, and had a height of around 164 feet (50m). It was built out of travertine, a type of limestone, extracted from the quarries near Tibur (Tivoli) and transported to Rome on

specially constructed roads that were some 20 feet (6m) wide. The stone blocks were held together by iron clamps once in situ but these were removed in the Middle Ages. Other materials used in the building work included bricks, tufa (porous limestone) blocks, and a type of concrete made from a mixture of small pieces of tufa and mortar. Walls were plastered and painted in red and white.

The exterior wall has four clearly defined stories, although the original Colosseum had only three. The lower three comprise a series of arches in different classical styles—the first are known as Tuscan Doric, the second Ionic, and the third Corinthian. The arches of the latter two levels once contained various statues. The fourth story was added by Emperor Alexander Severus (see below) and comprises slender Corinthian pilasters (imitations of a column). The upper story has a number of projecting corbels that once held 240 wooden spars. These were inserted through holes in the cornice, usually by sailors from the Roman fleet, so that they projected out over the arena. Awnings were then strung between the spars to give audiences respite from the afternoon heat of a summer's day.

Public entrance into the Colosseum was by numbered ticket via the ground floor, through any one of 76 arches numbered from I to LXXVI. and each measuring some 13 feet 9 inches (4m)

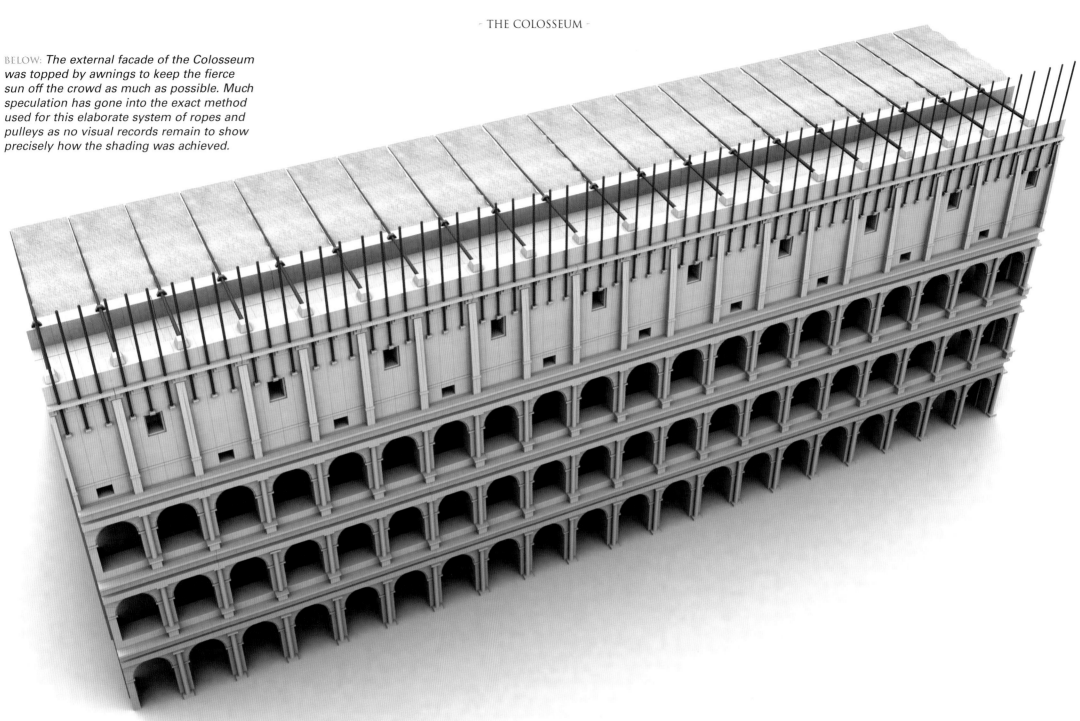

BELOW: *The external facade of the Colosseum was topped by awnings to keep the fierce sun off the crowd as much as possible. Much speculation has gone into the exact method used for this elaborate system of ropes and pulleys as no visual records remain to show precisely how the shading was achieved.*

LEFT: *Originally known as the* Amphitheatrum Flavium *(Flavium Amphitheater) the Roman Colosseum was built in the 70s* A.D. *and was the largest amphitheater built in the Roman Empire. It was built as an ellipse so that the crowd was as near the action as possible.*

wide and 23 feet 1 inch (7m) high. In addition there were four further entrances situated to the northeast, southeast, southwest, and northwest. These were reserved for members of the Roman nobility, especially that to the northeast which was for the emperor's personal use. Having walked through the appropriate archway, an ordinary ticket holder climbed the correct staircases to the appropriate level and passed through any one of many sloping passageways (*vomitoria*) and then found a seat.

The interior of the Colosseum has

suffered from the ravages of time and man but still presents a magnificent sight. The central arena, a rounded oval measuring some 250 feet (76m) by 144 feet (44m), consisted of wooden beams covered with up to six inches (15.2cm) of yellow sand. Indeed, arena is Latin for "sand" and it was chosen because of its ability to soak up blood. As all of the original flooring has disappeared bar a small reconstruction that was completed in 2000, modern viewers can see the complex of subterranean passageways, holding bays, and ramps that lie beneath the arena floor. These played a key role during the spectacles held in the

Colosseum—gladiators mustered there before fights; wild animals were kept behind bars before entering the arena by ramps that opened onto the floor of the arena; and items of scenery were both stored and lifted into view when needed. Originally, however, this area was built with a water system so that the arena above could be flooded to a depth of around five feet (1.5m) so that the crowds were able watch naval battles (*naumachiae*).

Seating arrangements in the Colosseum largely reflected Rome's social order, with the richer and more powerful being closer to the action than those of

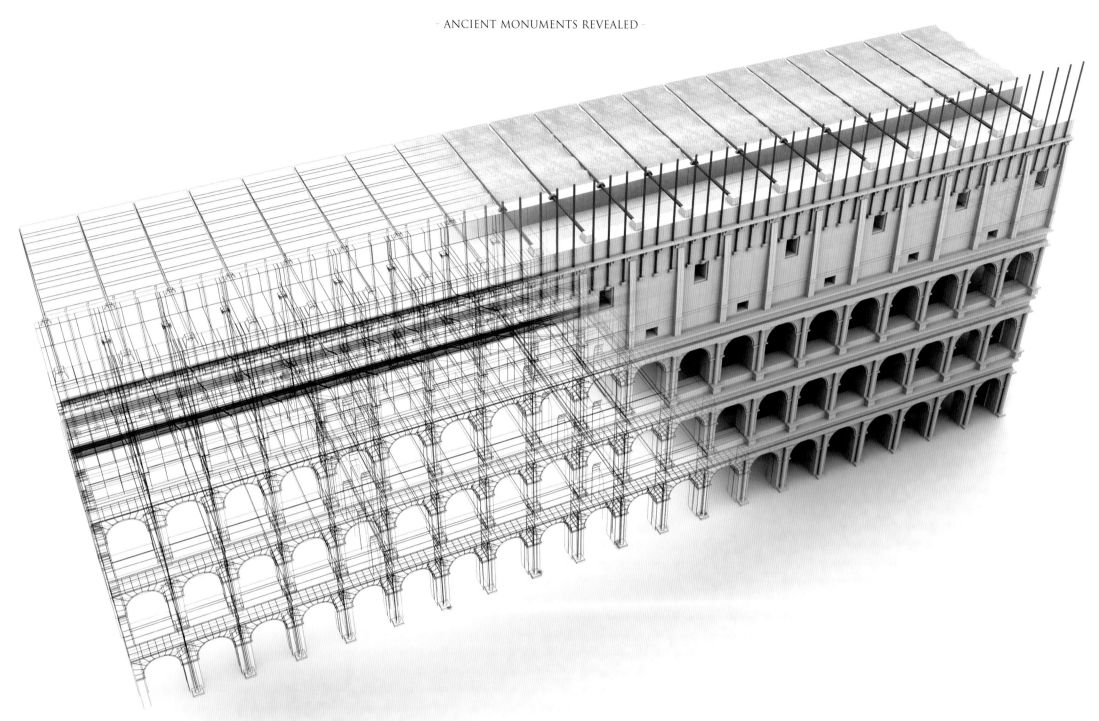

ABOVE: *The Colosseum was built in only eight years. It was started by Emperor Vespasian in 72 A.D., completed under Emperor Titus in 80 A.D., and improved by Emperor Domitian in 82 A.D.*

lesser status. The arena was enclosed by a wall some 13 feet (4m) high, chiefly to protect the onlookers from attack by wild animals, at the top of which was a wide parapeted terrace, the podium, the marble seats of which were reserved for the emperor, senators, pontiffs, major religious figures, and important foreign dignitaries. The emperor and his family took up the best viewing position, which was on the podium's north side. Rising behind the podium was the full range of the *cavea*, three tiers of seats (*maeniana*) in total. The first one rising immediately behind the podium was the reserve of *equites*

(knights) and consisted of 20 rows of seats. The second bank of 16 rows of seats was for *plebieans* (ordinary Roman citizens), while the third and highest tier was for the general, lesser public, including women and slaves. The former had access to seats but the latter had to stand. The lower two tiers were divided from each other and the podium by corridors (*praecinctiones*) enclosed by low walls, while the upper tier was separated from the second by a wall. Archaeologists estimate that the Colosseum could hold some 45,000 seated spectators and had standing room for a further 5,000.

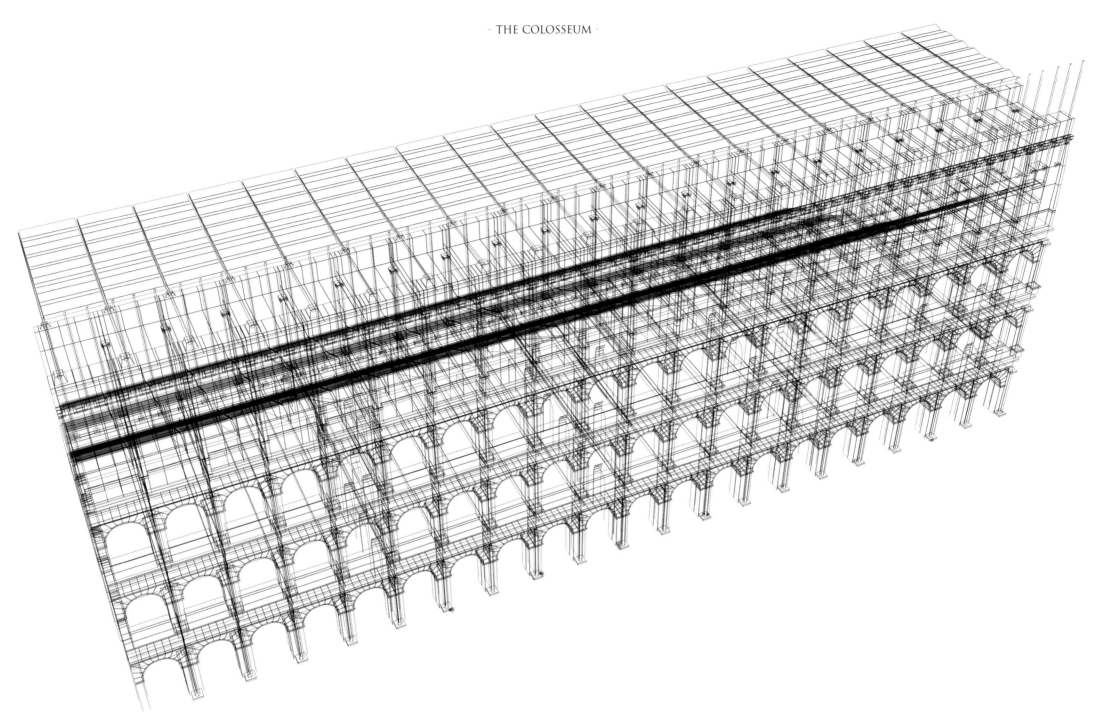

ABOVE: *On the ground floor are 80 archways with Doric columns. On the second floor the columns are Ionic and become Corinthian on the third level. The later addition of the fourth floor contained regular windows and the* velarium *(the awning) level.*

THE ARENA OF BLOODY SPECTACLES

The Colosseum was inaugurated in A.D. 80, although building work was still underway, and the lavish celebrations of that year set the tone for what was to follow over the next 500 or so. The various entertainments during the inaugural program continued for a staggering 100 days at the end of which 5,000 wild animals and an unrecorded number of gladiators had been killed for the delectation of the Roman populace. The games usually lasted from dawn to dusk but they occasionally carried on into the night under torch light.

Gladiators who fought in the Colosseum were mostly men who had been captured in battle or who had been condemned to death for major crimes. They were controlled by agents known as *procuratores*, who operated out of several barracks in the city. Once chosen the recruits were instructed by established gladiators and, depending on their abilities, were assigned various types of arms and equipment. Samnites, for example, used a sword and shield; Thracians carried a smaller sword and dagger; the *retiarii* carried a net and trident, the *secutor* a shield and sword, while the *murmillones* were identified by a helmet topped by a fish. Bouts in the arena might consists of gladiators with the same weapons being pitted against each other or, to make spectacles more interesting for the spectators, those with different weapons and fighting styles were matched.

Gladiator combat (*hoplomachia*) took several forms. First there were "pretend" contests in which the gladiators used muffled weapons to prevent serious injury. These contests were termed *lusio* if they filled the entire day or a week-long program or *prolusio* if they were merely preceding the real thing. This second form comprised either a series of duels to the death between pairs of gladiators or simultaneous combats between larger numbers of fighters. The various gladiators opened the day's events by parading around the arena accompanied by valets carrying their arms and equipment. After acknowledging the emperor with salutes and the phrase "Hail, emperor! Those about to die salute you," their weapons were checked to make sure they were suitably sharp, lots were drawn to see who fought whom, and the order to begin was given. Bouts were usually accompanied by a cacophony of sounds that mingled the crowds appreciative—or otherwise—roars with the noise of a band playing flutes, horns and trumpets.

If one gladiator was eventually killed, special attendants entered the arena, approached the body and then struck it on the forehead with a mallet to make sure that the stricken man was not feigning death. Assistants were then called in to remove the corpse on a stretcher while the attendants remained behind to clear away the blood by turning the sand. Other outcomes were possible, however. Sometimes gladiators were so evenly paired that they mortally wounded one another at the same time or fought to the point of exhaustion. In the latter case, the match was declared a draw and both men left the arena while the next pairing was called. Sometimes a badly though not

mortally wounded gladiator would put down his arms in submission, lie down on his back and extend his left arm asking for quarter. The final decision to kill or not rested with the victor, unless the emperor was present, and both might take advice from the baying of the crowd. A gladiator who had fought well and entertainingly might survive; one that had shown weakness or lack of skill would not. The most successful gladiators won fame and fortune—and the lucky few who survived down the years were granted a symbolic wooden sword (*rudis*), which indicated that they had finally won their freedom.

Although gladiatorial bouts were the most important type of entertainment in the Colosseum, they were usually interspersed with other forms to keep the crowds amused. The Colosseum also hosted other events, such as chariot races (*ludi circenses*), *silvae* in which mock forests and glades were inhabited by wild animals, and dramas that re-enacted mythological tales. Animal spectacles, known as *venationes*, came in several forms, from the simply entertaining to the outright barbaric. Tame but invariably exotic animals, such as elephants, lions, and tigers, often entered the arena to perform tricks as if in a modern circus. Thereafter blood was spilt. Wild animals were often pitted against each other, fighting to the death, or the action might be spiced up with the addition of an execution of a condemned man. Contrary to popular belief, there is no evidence that early Christians were martyred in the arena.

The animal bouts might consist of the same animals—say buffalo against buffalo—fighting but more often than not they pitted different species against each other, such as an elephant against a rhinoceros. Next came one-sided contests in which animals in the arena were simply targeted by archers from the safety of the podium or other protected areas. Finally, there were direct contests between man and beast. *Bestiarii*, men armed with spears, flaming torches, bows, and daggers, and frequently accompanied by

LEFT AND RIGHT: *How the awning is thought to have been deployed during the heat of the day to provide cool breezes. On the fourth floor 240 sturdy wooden poles (*piles*) held shading blinds made from linen. Known as the* velarium, *the awning was controlled by a detachment of the Imperial navy sailors from the port of Misenum. When they were needed for the games, the sailors were stationed in a barracks nearby so as to be on hand for awning duty—for either rain or sunshine. Standing on special platforms they followed shouted orders to work the ropes. When fully out the awning could cover about two thirds of the arena.*

LEFT: *The Colosseum has survived three major earthquakes—in 422, 1231, and 1349—its resilience is believed to be thanks to the 43ft deep concrete platform on which it sits.*

BELOW: *The stepped seating, known as the* cavea, *was divided into five sections each of which was strictly defined by social class. The first and most prestigious row was the podium and limited to senators, and included the emperor's marble box. The second row, the* maenianum primum, *was reserved for Roman aristocrats who were not in the senate. The third rank, the* maenianum secundum *was subdivided into three sections: the lowest, the* immum *was for wealthy citizens. Above them in the* summum *were the poor citizens, while the third, wooden section, the* maenianum secundum in legneis *was added by Emperor Domitian for women and slaves.*

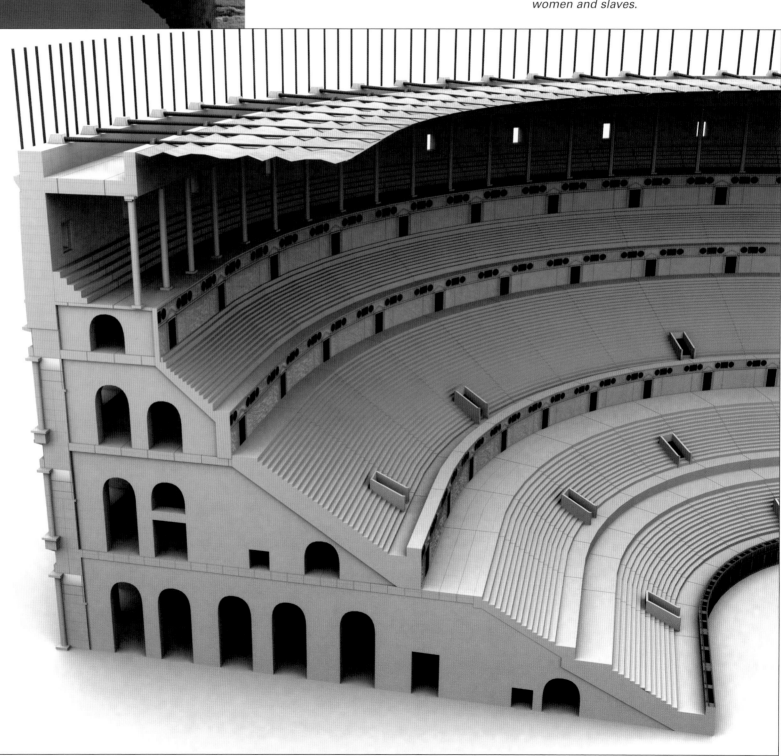

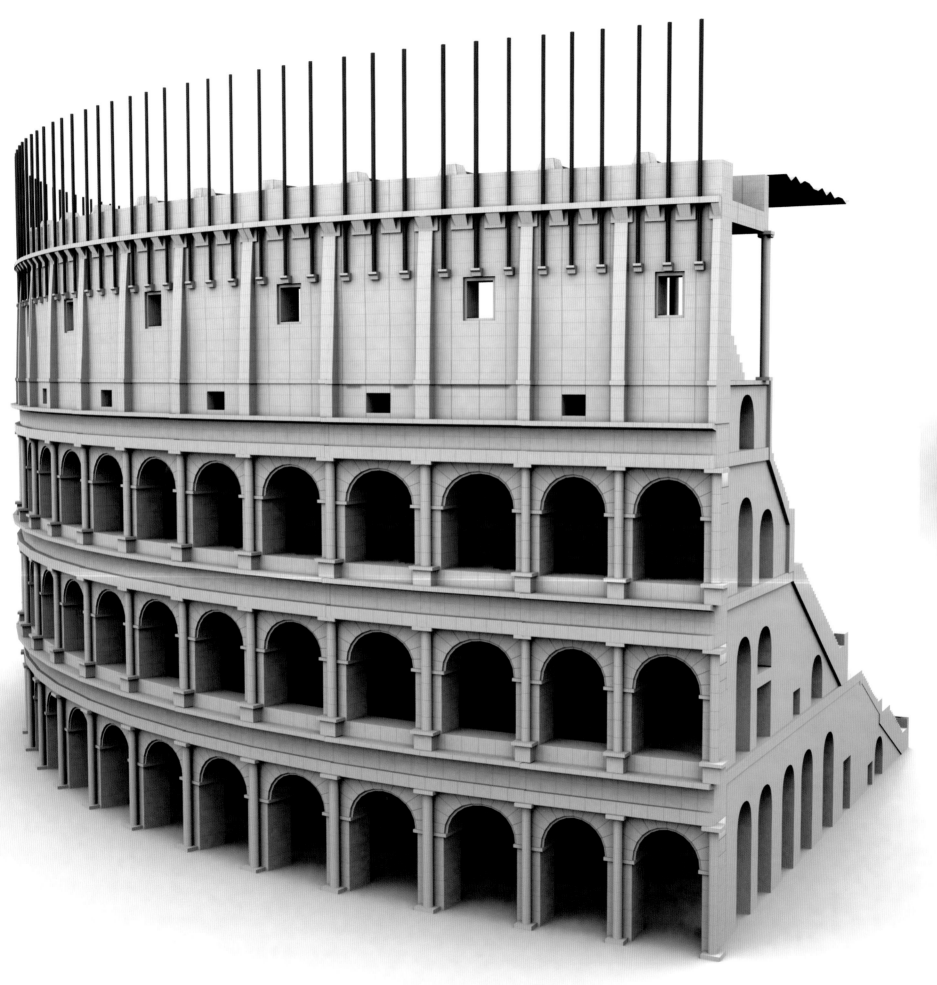

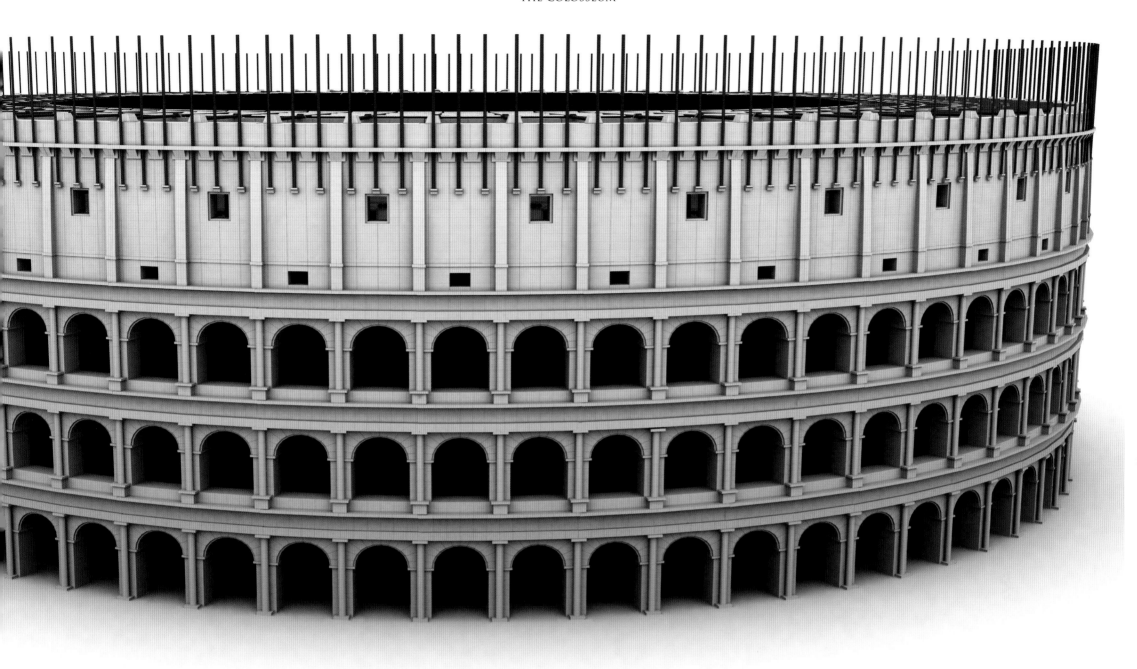

ABOVE AND LEFT: *The Colosseum was originally built to contain 50,000 spectators and cleverly designed to get the public in and out quickly. It had 80 ground level entrances, two of which were reserved for the gladiators and two for the Imperial family. Spectators were each given a numbered pottery shard with their section and seat number on it. They got to their seats via numbered stairways and numbered* vomitoria *(passageways). These were designed so that the entire Colosseum could fill in fifteen minutes and empty in five.*

packs of hunting dogs, took on a variety of wild animals, especially members of the big cat family. The scale of slaughter was so immense that many of the animals disappeared from the Roman Empire.

THE LATER COLOSSEUM

In many respects it is remarkable that the ruins of the amphitheater that visitors flock to today are as well preserved as they are, as the Colosseum has suffered various indignities down the centuries. It suffered serious fire damage in A.D. 217 but was restored by Emperor Alexander Severus, who ruled between A.D. 222 and A.D. 235.

Its fortunes improved for a while and in A.D. 248 the amphitheater hosted the 1,000th anniversary celebrations to commemorate the founding of Rome. Some 1,000 pairs of gladiators took part in the events and 32 elephants, 50 lions, and 12 tigers were slaughtered.

Such spectacles were eventually outlawed in part due to the spread of Christianity throughout the empire that was recognized by Emperor Constantine I (A.D. 306–337). He was a joint signatory to the Edict of Milan in A.D. 313 that guaranteed freedom of Christian worship throughout his domain. Equally important was the

sheer cost of such events. As Rome's power declined, the empire's coffers were far too overstretched by the need to combat external threats to support such costly spectacles. Gladiatorial combat was subsequently forbidden by the Western Roman Emperor Flavius Honorius in A.D. 404 and fights between wild animals were phased out in the early sixth century. Nature also conspired against the Colosseum and it suffered earthquake damage on at least three occasions— A.D. 443, after which it was probably restored, as well as 1231 and 1349. The amphitheater was later converted into a

BELOW: *Thanks to the open nature of the Colosseum it was considered a good place for meeting the opposite sex.*

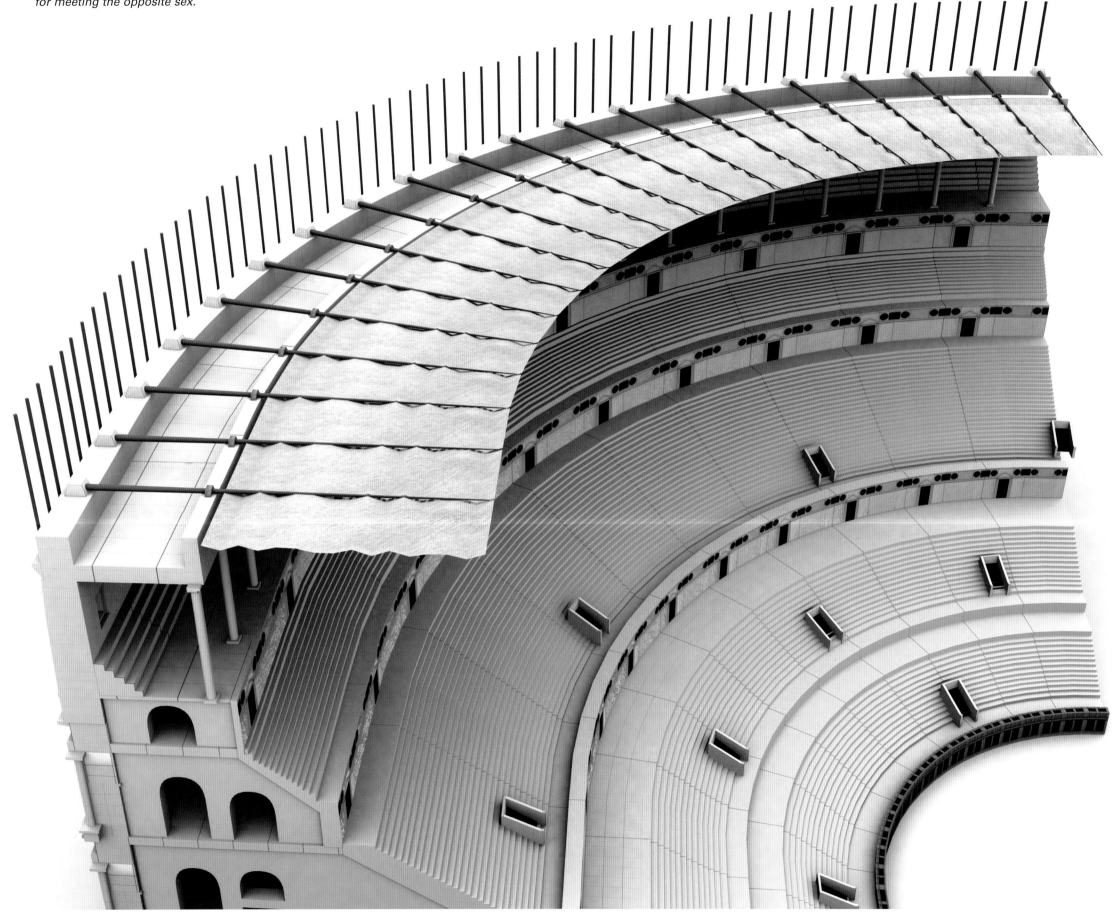

ABOVE: *For centuries Roman builders have plundered the Colosseum for stone which they then used for building—including St Peter's cathedral and many Roman palaces belonging to the nobility. The original marble facade was either taken for building work or burned to make quicklime. This desecration only stopped in 1749 when Pope Benedict XIV forbade the taking of stone from the Colosseum declaring it a holy building and consecrating it to the Passion of Christ in memory of the many Christian martyrs who died there—although in fact most of them died in the Circus Maximus rather than here.*

castle by two of Rome's leading families, the Frangipani and the Annibaldi, during a period of political and religious unrest in the twelfth and thirteenth centuries.

The Holy Roman Emperor Henry VII (1274–1313) made a gift of the Colosseum to the senate and people of Rome in 1312 but neither made any particular efforts to preserve the remains. By the fifteenth century it was in even greater peril, not least because it was being used as a quarry. The valuable travertine blocks were used in the construction of several major buildings in

the capital, including the Palazzo di Cancelleria, the Palazzo Barberini, the Palazzo di Venezia, and St. Peter's. Hope returned in the guise of a series of heads of the Roman Catholic faith. Benedict XIV (pope between 1740 and 1758) dedicated the Colosseum to the Passion of Jesus in 1749, stating that it was sanctified by the blood of the early Christian martyrs, although there is no evidence to suggest that Christians were put to death in the amphitheater. A succession of popes in the nineteenth century, chiefly Pius VII (1800–1823), Leo XII

ABOVE AND RIGHT: *The architects responsible for the Colosseum belonged to the imperial family of Quintus Aterius. The Colosseum got its name from a colossal bronze statue of Emperor Nero, which was reportedly 115ft high. This had been moved on the orders of Emperor Hadrian from the vestibule of the Nero's Golden House to the square in front of the arena by 24 elephants, to make way for the Temple of Venus and Rome.*

ABOVE: *The Colosseum as it is today is remarkably intact. The interior has largely collapsed exposing some of the network of subterranean passages. Originally a movable wooden floor covered the arena and* contained numerous trap doors and huge hinged platforms (called hegmata) *to enable animal cages and large pieces of scenery to be lifted into the arena.*

ABOVE: *Emperor Domitian ordered the improvement of the Colosseum (after only two years) with a two-level subterranean holding area (the* hypogeum*) of cages, rooms, and tunnels to house the gladiators and wild animals ready for the battles.*

(1823–1829), Gregory XVI (1831–1846) and Pius IX (1846–1878), undertook various remedial works, chiefly the building of buttresses and other supports to prevent the collapse of its walls.

Major efforts to preserve and enhance the Colosseum were made in the final decade of the nineteenth century, between 1893 and 1896, when Guido Baccelli cleared obtrusive buildings from around the site, and this work continued in 1933 during the construction of the Via del Fori Imperiali. In reality, restoration and preservation work is virtually never-ending and continues to the present day. The Colosseum, which continues to attract hundreds of thousands of visitors each year, is open from 9 am to one hour before dusk in summer and from 9am to 5.30pm in winter, although it is closed for Christmas and New Year's Day.

RIGHT AND FAR RIGHT: *This reconstruction of the Colosseum shows the wall between the arena and the audience, the great boxes for the imperial family and other grandees, and the awning in place.*

BELOW: *The external facade was originally clad with marble. It is a remarkably modern building that was the forerunner of the sporting arenas we use for major events today.*

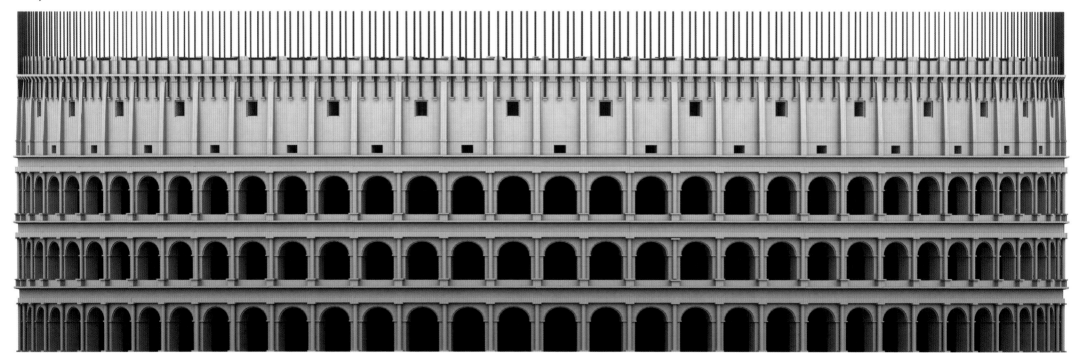

THIS PAGE: *The gladiators' entrance into the arena: over the years several hundred thousand people perished here during the games and similar numbers of animals. The Colosseum was inaugurated with 100 days of games during which a reported 5,000 animals alone were slaughtered.*

RIGHT: *The arena could be flooded so that impressive naval battles—called* naumachiae *—could be staged. The water was held in a large subterranean tank which was connected to an aqueduct and piped in through tunnels as required. The water emptied via the city's sewerage system.*

BELOW: *A gladiator's eye view of the emperor's marble clad imperial box. Their salute to the Caesars is remembered down the years: "Morituri te salutant!" ("Those who are about to die salute you!") In fact, as with so many such legends, there is little to suggest that gladiators habitually said this before combat. The only record is in Suetonius's life of the Emperor Claudius (ruled A.D. 41–54). It happened before a mock naval battle on Lake Fucinus in A.D. 52. Claudius is reported to have answered "Aut non" ("Or not") whereupon the gladiators refused to fight, saying the emperor had pardoned them. They were finally induced to battle when Claudius himself talked them into it. However, Hollywood liked the idea and so the myth has been perpetuated.*

CHAPTER V
MESA VERDE

MESA VERDE

THE GREAT CLIFF DWELLINGS OF THE ANASAZI

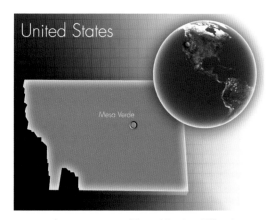

ABOVE: *Locator map–Mesa Verde cliff palace in New Mexico, U.S.*

PREVIOUS PAGE: *The largest cliff dwelling in North America, Mesa Verde is now contained in the Mesa Verde National Park.*

RIGHT: *Spruce Tree House is another cliff dwelling—at Chapin Mesa in Mesa Verde National Park. It was built between 1200 and 1276 and contained 114 rooms and eight ceremonial kivas, housing about 100 people.*

The much-photographed Cliff Palace complex, which is now part of Colorado's Mesa Verde National Park, is one of the many great architectural achievements of the Anasazi, a Native American people who inhabited the so-called Four Corners Region—that today takes in parts of Arizona, Colorado, New Mexico, and Utah—for more than 1,000 years.

The Anasazi people (the name means ancient ones or ancient foreigners in the Navajo language) began to develop a distinctive culture around 100 B.C. and they enjoyed local pre-eminence between A.D. 900 and 1300 by which time their influence had spread across much of what in now the southwest United States. They began to settle in the Mesa Verde (Green Table) region from around A.D.500 and occupied various locations across the deeply dissected uplands for the next 800 years or so. Archaeologists have identified some 4,000 Anasazi-related sites in the national park (there are undoubtedly more) and have estimated that the Anasazi population peaked at around 30,000 inhabitants.

WHO WERE THE ANASAZI?

The earliest Anasazi were primarily hunter-gathers but they were also renowned for their intricate weaving of food containers, sandals and various other practical and decorative items from the area's readily available rushes, straw, vines and yucca plants. Archaeologists now term the first

but still little-known Anasazi period as Archaic but subsequent generations have been termed Basketmaker due to their early proficiency in weaving such objects. They also developed a settled form of agriculture over time and, as this occupation became increasingly important to them, the Anasazi adopted a more sedentary way of life. They began building semi-permanent rounded and domed buildings of wood and mud positioned over shallow holes in the ground.

These simple structures gradually developed into deeper pit houses that were used as living quarters until around A.D. 750 when the Anasazi began to build a new style of dwelling, although they retained the circular pit houses (also known as *kiva*) for ceremonial and social occasions. Kivas derive their name from the Hopi Native American word for ceremonial room and they were roofed over with beams and mud supported on pilasters. Entry was by way of a ladder through a hole cut into the center of the roof and a small hole in the middle of the floor, known as a *sipapu*, was meant to symbolize the entrance to the underworld.

The new buildings, which heralded what has been termed the "Golden Age" of the Anasazi, were radically different from what had gone before and consisted of stone and mud mortar (*adobe*) walls with beams supporting roofs constructed out of sticks, grass and mud. The new

building style has been named "pueblo," after the Spanish for a town or community, and this was what the increasingly settled Anasazi gradually developed. What began as simple single-story and single-room constructions of the Pueblo I era evolved over the next 250 years or so; first, into larger one-family homes and second, into more complex multiple-occupancy and multi-level square or rounded structures.

The latter, usually known as "Great Houses," comprised numerous rooms with shared walls built one above the other and connected by simple wooden ladders. As each story was ranged back from that below, the roof of one story acted as a terrace-like feature to the one above. Rooms measured on average six feet (2m) by eight feet (2.4m) and probably housed no more than two or three people. The terraces outside were where pots were made, tools fashioned out of stone, wood, and bone, and baskets (of declining quality during this period) woven. The Anasazis' crowning achievement during this Pueblo II era was Pueblo Bonito, the largest of thirteen villages in the Chaco Canyon. Build in the early tenth century in what is now New Mexico, the settlement is a semi-circular masonry design linked by a straight wall. Within the walls are 800 rooms spread across five stories, various storage pits and numerous kivas.

LEFT: *Cliff Palace is an ancient settlement in Chapin Mesa. It was built between 1190 and 1280 and inhabited by around 100 people. It is the largest cliff dwelling in North America and is now protected within Mesa Verde National Park in southwest Colorado.*

BELOW: *There are 23 kivas in Cliff Palace, one of which is more or less central to the buildings. The entire structure is separated by a series of partition walls which have no doorways or holes to get to the other side; this seems to confirm archaeologists' suspicions that two separate communities lived here and that they only met at the central kiva whose walls are plastered with a different color on either side.*

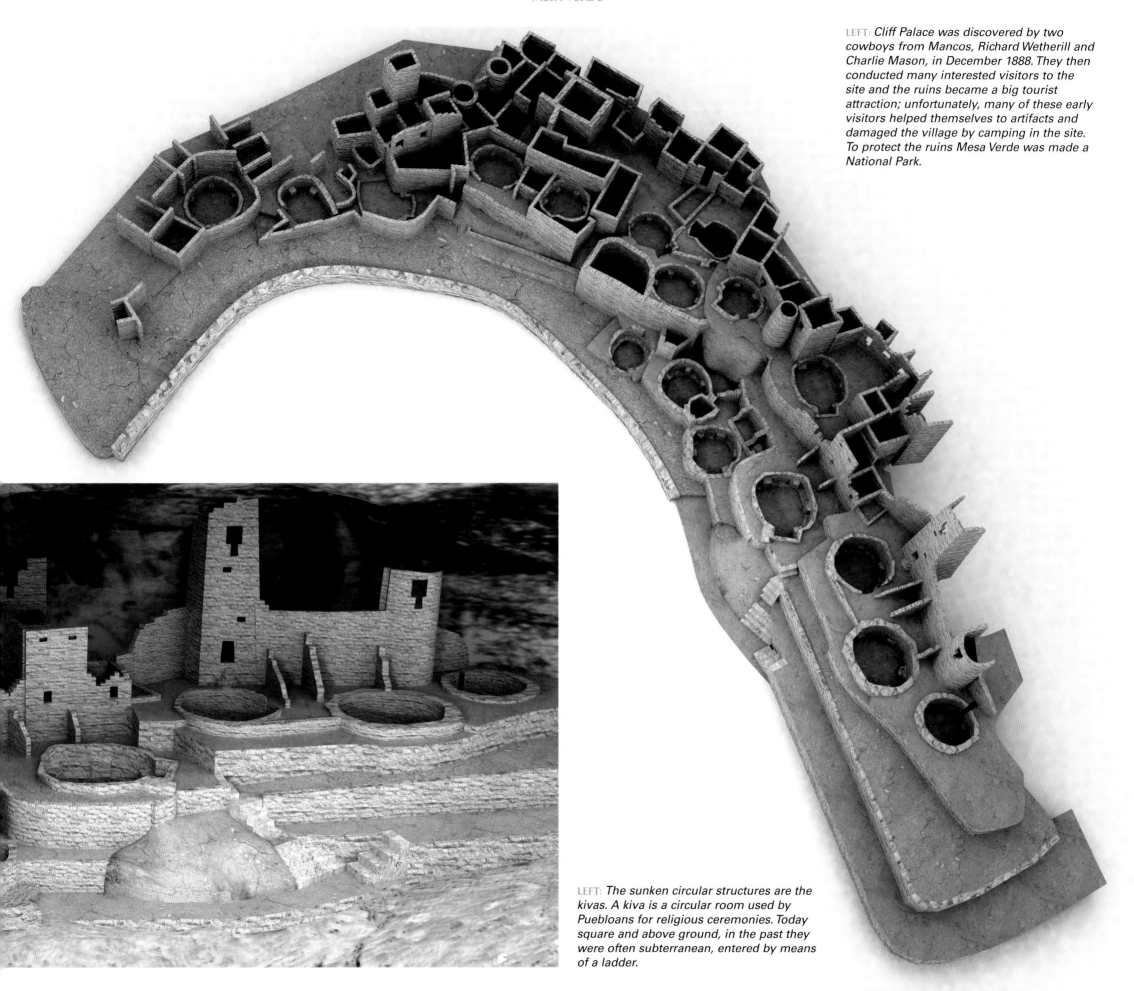

LEFT: *Cliff Palace was discovered by two cowboys from Mancos, Richard Wetherill and Charlie Mason, in December 1888. They then conducted many interested visitors to the site and the ruins became a big tourist attraction; unfortunately, many of these early visitors helped themselves to artifacts and damaged the village by camping in the site. To protect the ruins Mesa Verde was made a National Park.*

LEFT: *The sunken circular structures are the kivas. A kiva is a circular room used by Puebloans for religious ceremonies. Today square and above ground, in the past they were often subterranean, entered by means of a ladder.*

ABOVE: *Mesa Verde National Park contains around 600 dwellings constructed by the Northern San Juan Anasazi culture. The buildings were constructed between A.D. 1200 and 1300 but soon abandoned by their inhabitants.*

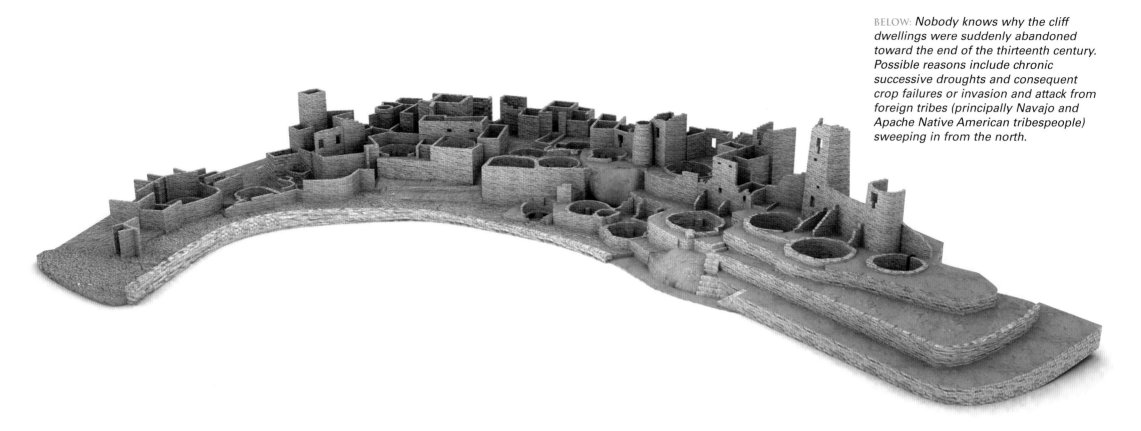

BELOW: *Nobody knows why the cliff dwellings were suddenly abandoned toward the end of the thirteenth century. Possible reasons include chronic successive droughts and consequent crop failures or invasion and attack from foreign tribes (principally Navajo and Apache Native American tribespeople) sweeping in from the north.*

The agricultural system practiced by the Anasazi also became more sophisticated during this era. Many of their settlements were built on the tops of the region's mesas (plateaux) and they grew their crops nearby, often on terraced fields irrigated by a system of reservoirs and channels. They mainly cultivated beans, corn, and squash, food that was supplemented by hunting deer, rabbits, and other forms of wild game. They had few domesticated animals, just dogs and turkeys. Greater farming efficiency led to larger surpluses of food that allowed some Anasazi to developed various other skills, including fine pottery making. Trade also became increasingly important to them and there is evidence that routes stretched as far as the Pacific coast and the Gulf of Mexico. Yet for all the Anasazis' seeming success during the Pueblo II period, their way of life suffered a dramatic collapse during the second half of the twelfth century. It is generally considered that the chief culprit was a period of drought between 1140 and 1190 but other suggestions put forward have

included anything from disease to warfare.

The Anasazis' response to the crisis varied. In the subsequent Pueblo III age some continued to live in modified versions of the great houses but others developed a new style of living, preferring to build their settlements not on the tops of the mesas as before but rather in the large, overhung recesses in the plateaux's steep-sided canyons' cliffs. Various reasons have been given for the switch to the new locations. Some commentators have suggest that places like Mesa Verde's Cliff Palace, the most spectacular of these recess dwellings, were so placed to protect their inhabitants from the region's harsh climate, while others have argued that the new sites offered better protection against marauders and raiders.

THE OCCUPATION OF CLIFF PALACE
The Anasazi of the Pueblo III era continued to build on an equally impressive scale in many instances. Their crowning glory, Cliff Palace, is situated in

a sandstone cliff in what is now known as Chapin Mesa and is thought to have had residential, administrative, and ceremonial functions. Dendrochronology (the analysis of tree growth rings) indicates that the palace was built and updated over a considerable period, from around 1190 to 1260, but that most of the major building work was undertaken in a single 20-year period. The natural recess that shelters the palace is some 89 feet (27m) deep and 59 feet (18m) high and the buildings themselves stretch for around 288 feet (88m).

The construction methods employed and materials used on the project were nothing out of the ordinary to the Anasazi. The builders used sandstone blocks shaped to size by using harder stones taken from nearby rivers; adobe mortar comprising water, soil, and ash; and locally sourced wood. They also fitted smaller pieces of stone, a process known as "chinking," into the mortar. This procedure had two main functions—to fill in any gaps and to add structural cohesion to the walls. There is evidence that many walls were finished

with a thin wash of plaster on to which abstract designs were drawn. Much of this decorative work has been eroded away over time but the best preserved remains are today found in the interior of the four-story tower at the southern end of the complex.

The palace is a labyrinth of some 150 rooms over various sizes and shapes spread over several levels. The presence of fire hearths in just 25 to 30 of them suggests that many of the rooms were simply used for crop storage or for other as yet unknown purposes. Archaeologists have identified nine definite storage rooms for crops in the upper reaches of the palace that could only be accessed by removable ladders, and where the crops would be safe from moisture damage or rodent attack. Aside from storage and living rooms, the complex contains 23 sunken circular kivas. Perhaps surprisingly for such a densely occupied settlement, it has no immediate water supply and the occupants had probably to meet their needs from springs on the other side of the canyon, below the Sun Temple, which has an

astronomical alignment for ceremonial purposes.

Archaeologists estimate that the site was inhabited by between 100 and 150 Anasazi. Extrapolating from the palace's low doorways, the evidence suggests that the menfolk of Cliff Palace reached an average height of around 5 feet 5 inches (1.63m), while the womenfolk were some 5 inches (3.6cm) shorter. The Anasazi had short lifespans compared to those of today, with most dying in their early 30s, although some may had lived into their 50 and 60s. Infant mortality rates were also extremely

high, with around 50 percent of children dying before the age of five.

Although Cliff Palace is the largest of the such dwelling complexes, Mesa Verde contains several others, although virtually none is on the same scale. In total, the modern park contains nearly 600 cliff dwellings with some 75 percent of them consisting of just one to five rooms—but there are exceptions. To the northeast of the palace lies Spruce Tree House (see photograph on page 113), which was built into a recess some 90 feet (27m) deep and 200 feet (61m) wide. The site consists of

ABOVE AND RIGHT: *Cliff Palace comprises a dense cluster of buildings constructed under a protective overhang of the steep canyon sides in a finger of Chapin Mesa overlooking Cliff Canyon. The alcove is 262ft (80m) long and 66ft (20m) deep and the village is built direct on the sloping floor at 6,790ft (2,270m) above sea level. It was built in haphazard style as needs dictated rather than to an organized plan. The surrounding trees are mostly pinyon and juniper.*

LEFT AND BELOW: *The first dwellings were built at the back of the overhang but as newer buildings were constructed these became store rooms. Flat courtyards were cut out from the stone underneath as were circular subterranean kivas that were used as meeting places for the menfolk of the clan. Over time the roofs have collapsed leaving the rooms open to the elements.*

eight kivas and 114 rooms in total that were home to an estimated 100 Anasazis

The glory days of Cliff Palace and the area's other Pueblo III settlements did not last for long, and the Anasazi gradually left the Mesa Verde region during the latter part of the thirteenth century so that by 1300 most of the dwellings and associated features had been abandoned.

Archaeologists have long been puzzled by this sudden and dramatic shift in fortune and have suggested various reasons for the Anasazis' mass exodus. Tellingly, there is strong evidence generated by dendrochronology of a major lack of water between 1276 and 1299, the so-called "Great Drought" that may have brought about the collapse of their agricultural

system. Yet other commentators have pointed out that the Anasazi had survived other periods of such shortage. Others have identified attacks by nomadic raiders such as the Apaches and Ute or even infighting between the Anasazi themselves as reasons for the collapse. Acute shortages of raw materials, especially wood for fuel and building work, and

disease have also been suggested as causes for the abandonment of Mesa Verde.

Whatever the background to the migration, it appears that the Anasazi mostly moved to the south during this era of crisis, chiefly along the Rio Grande and Little Colorado Rivers, where they established new settlements but not on

BELOW: *Cliff Palace was the second cliff dwelling in Mesa Verde to be excavated and partially restored (in 1909) with the repair of wall foundations and the reconstruction of part of the four-story tower. The buildings were identified as being for secular—ie living —use, or for ceremonial purposes. Numerous pieces of broken pottery were unearthed, again both apparently from secular and ceremonial objects.*

RIGHT: *When the site was first properly investigated in 1891 the complete absence of structural wood was remarked on—and was conjectured to be a reason for the abandonment of the settlement.*

the spectacular scale of what had gone before and not in the style of Cliff Palace. Over time the Anasazis' cultural traits were pass on to their descendants, the modern-day Pueblo Native Americans and, in acknowledgment of this, the later Anasazi are now more commonly referred to as the Ancestral Puebloans.

THE MODERN PARK

The architectural treasure trove of Mesa Verde was "lost" to the outside world for around 600 years but in 1849–1850 a U.S. Army lieutenant stumbled on some of its structures. The first partial survey of the site was made in 1874, but it perhaps surprisingly failed to find Cliff Palace. The chief figure in this first major exploration was photographer W. H. Jackson of the U.S. Geological and Geographical Survey but he named just one Pueblo building, Two-Story Cliff in Marcos Canyon.

The Cliff Palace complex was actually rediscovered by chance in December 1888, when two local cattlemen from the nearby town of Marcos, Richard Wetherill and his brother-in-law Charlie Mason, came across its well-preserved ruins on the 18th while searching for cattle scattered by a recent heavy snowfall. For the next eighteen years they exploited the site largely for their own benefit, guiding increasing numbers of visitors and archaeologists, both amateur and professional, through the ruins and, more worryingly, allowing artifacts such as the Anasazis' distinctive black-and-white pottery to be looted or sent overseas.

Attempts to save Mesa Verde for the nation began thanks to a campaign led by Virginia McClurg of Colorado Springs, who was shocked by the steady loss of artifacts, and the area finally won National Park status was on June 29, 1906, a development that made it the first and the only one in the United States dedicated to pre-Columbian archaeological remains. Congress also passed the Antiquities Act that gave protected status to any artifacts found on federal land the same year to put a final stop to the unregulated export of invaluable and irreplaceable national

ABOVE: *From what little tree ring evidence was available, Cliff Palace been dated to the thirteenth century. By counting the number of suites of rooms clustered around a single courtyard, archaeologists have concluded that Cliff Palace held a permanent population of 25 households.*

RIGHT: *It is thought that kivas were used for ceremonial purposes but that at times of special ceremonies, when the population of the village swelled, they were also used as temporary sleeping quarters for the visitors.*

treasures. Cliff Palace, which had suffered somewhat from looting and vandalism since its discovery in 1888, was first stabilized and excavated by Jesse Walter Fewkes of the Smithsonian Institute in 1909. Mesa Verde has been under almost constant analysis and examination since Fewkes' first really professional archaeological expedition.

The modern park, which actually occupies the northernmost part of Mesa Verde, covers an area of some 81 square miles (208sq km), with many of the major archaeological sites situated to the southwest dotted among the valleys, cliff sides, and heights of the Wetherill and Chapin Mesas. Cliff Palace itself lies in the latter area, along with other notable remains including Cedar Tree Tower, Spruce Tree House, Square Tower House, and Balcony House. Despite the impact of Wetherill and Chapin, Mesa Verde as a whole is the best-preserved collection of archaeological remains in the modern United States in part thanks to its very isolation and in part due to the efforts of Virginia McClurg and others. Chapin Mesa is the jewel in the park's crown as it contains the greatest concentration of Anasazi-related buildings, but it is also worth visiting Wetherill Mesa, which contains the Long House, the second largest cliff dwelling in the park. These various sites reflect all of the stages of the Anasazis' occupation of the region from their earliest pit houses through above-ground villages and towns to the final imposing multiroom structures that, like Cliff Palace, are found in the mesas' cliff recesses.

However, the park is much more than just a collection of structures and archaeologists have also discovered many

LEFT: *Cliff Palace is the largest of the cliff dwelling villages. One of the biggest perennial problems for the villagers would have been getting access to water. There is no water source at the settlement, instead the villages would have had to collect it from the bottom of the canyon, possibly from a well.*

RIGHT: *Entrance to a kiva in the cliff dwelling ruins at Mesa Verde.*

ABOVE: *Interior of an Anasazi cliff dwelling. Five types of secular room have been identified in Mesa Verde cliff dwellings: living rooms, eating rooms, food granaries, non-food storage rooms, and open unroofed areas. In addition they have a number of rooms whose function is not known or understood.*

LEFT: *The interior of a cliff dwelling. For five centuries the Mesa Verde area was occupied by Pueblo Indian farmers but suddenly in the thirteenth century they moved their homes from the open farmland to the shelter and security of cliff dwellings deep in the canyons. Then they suddenly left, abandoning the villages and their farmlands.*

day-to-day items relating to the Anasazis' culture such as jewelry, items of cotton and feather clothing and the distinctive black and white pottery that first emerged around A.D. 900. Thanks to the arid climate of the southwest, many fine examples of the Anasazis' basketwork have also been discovered. Examples of all of these finds can be found at the Chapin Mesa Museum, which lies some two miles (3.2km) northwest of Cliff Palace and is open all year round, albeit with slightly reduced opening times between October and May.

The park's other facilities are mostly open from late spring to early fall, and these are the best times to visit as soaring summer temperatures and deep snow in winter make the going difficult for all but

the hardiest. Visitors should also note than a small charge is made for a guided tour of Cliff Palace, which is open from 9am to 5pm daily except during winter. Tickets can be purchased from the Far View Visitors Center, which lies southwest of the park's main entrance and a short distance to the north of Cliff Palace.

The park receives some 600,000 visitors each year and its significance to humankind was recognized on September 8, 1978, when UNESCO granted it World Cultural Heritage Site status. Major celebrations took place on June 29, 2006, to celebrate Mesa Verde's centennial.

FAR LEFT: *A sunbeam shines through the square opening in the roof of a kiva at Spruce Tree House. This dwelling was built around A.D. 1200 and in 1908 it became the first of the dwellings to be excavated. A number of the artifacts found here were sent to the Smithsonian Institution. There are 15 rooms to every kiva in this settlement.*

LEFT: *A spiral petroglyph (c. 100–1300) decorates a wall of Pipe Shrine House which is located in Far View settlement in the upper portion of Chapin Mesa. This was one of around 50 villages all clustered within a one and a half mile square area and probably occupied from A.D. 900 to 1300. Pipe Shrine House was excavated and stabilized in 1922. The dwelling was named Pipe Shrine House after the dozen decorated ceremonial clay pipes found in the pit in the kiva. Archaeologists believe that this was a ceremonial building rather than a dwelling.*

CHAPTER VI
CHICHEN ITZA

CHICHEN ITZA

HIGHLIGHT OF THE MAYAN CLASSIC PERIOD

ABOVE: *Locator map–Chichen Itza is in the Yucatan peninsula, Mexico.*

PREVIOUS PAGE: *Chichen Itza has been extensively explored since the nineteenth century, with detailed archaeological work by the Carnegie Institute in 1924–1936. Today Mexican archaeologists are involved in a long-term research program.*

RIGHT: *Chichen Itza was built by the Mayans in around A.D. 800 but was not discovered by Europeans until around 1566. The name comes from* chi *(mouth),* chen *(source), and* Itza *(tribal name). In an area of around eight square miles are the remains of 200 or so buildings. About 30 have been restored.*

The largely restored remains of the city-state of Chichen Itza (Mouth of the Well of the Itzaes), which can be found in the north of Mexico's Yucatan Peninsula, are without doubt the most impressive monuments to the building abilities of the ancient Mayan civilization.

The greater part of the ancient city lies to the south of the *Cenote Sagrado* (Sacred Cenote), a large natural well, and contains limestone temple-pyramids, ballcourts, platforms and other structures closely tied to Mayan religious beliefs and rituals that were centered on ritual human sacrifice. The height of Chichen Itza's influence and power stretched from around A.D. 800 to 1200.

THE DEVELOPMENT OF CHICHEN ITZA

It is generally agreed that there were three distinct phases of settlement at Chichen Itza. The first two are usually put together and referred to as *Chichen Viejo* (Old Chichen) or the Maya Phase, and the first settlers to reach at the site are thought to have arrived round A.D. 700, when the Mayan civilization based in what is now the Mexican state of Chiapas and neighboring Guatamala was at its height in the so-called Maya Classic Period. It is possible that the first settlers were attracted to the site because of two natural wells, which are known as the Cenote Xtoloc and Cenote Sagrado (Sacred). The former was named after the Mayan lizard god and provided the city with water,

while the latter had religious importance (see below). Many archaeologists, but not all, believe that the Maya of the Classic Period created Chichen Viejo. The second period of the Maya Phase began around A.D. 900, a time commonly known as the Maya Post-Classic Period, and this saw the building of some of Chichen Itza's first great buildings, such as the inner pyramid of *El Castillo* (The Castle).

The third phase of the site's development is known as *Chichen Nuevo* (New Chichen) or the Toltec-Maya Phase and is thought to have begun in the eleventh century, when the Itza, a Mayan people from Tabasco, arrived. Academics have disagreed over what happened next. An increasing minority believes that Toltecs of the city-state of Tula moved into the Yucatan and overran the more peaceful Mayans' towns and villages, bringing with them the cult of Quetzalcoatl, the feathered serpent that became known to the Maya as Kukulcan. The majority disputes this aggressive occupation theory, arguing that Chichen Itza was a center of both trade and ideas and that the Maya simply incorporated Toltec beliefs into their own culture. To confuse matters further, some commentators have argued that the presumed Toltec religious and architectural features at Chichen Itza actually predate those at Tula, thus suggesting that it was the Maya that influenced the Toltecs rather than vice-versa.

Whichever view is correct, the Toltec-Maya Phase saw the construction of several impressive structures, including El Castillo and the *Templo de Guerros* (Temple of the Warriors). Chichen Itza reached its greatest power during this era and in the twelfth century it established and dominated the Mayapan League, a confederation of the other Mayan cities in Yucatan. It is thought that around 90 percent of the Maya were farmers and workers, ruled over by the other 10 percent, who were nobles, priests, and warriors. Chichen Itza's power gradually waned and the site was largely abandoned by 1461 during a conflict with the rival city-state of Mayapan. There is evidence that Chichen Itza remained a site of religious activity until well after the arrival of the Spanish conquistadores in 1519 but it certainly descended into further ruin over the following centuries.

THE REMAINS OF OLD CHICHEN

Chichen Viejo lies roughly 500 yards (457m) to the south of Chichen Nuevo but it is less well known and is still undergoing study and restoration. Archaeologists first thought that the settlement was occupied before the founding of Chichen Nuevo but are now satisfied that both were in use at roughly the same time. The site is much less accessible that Chichen Nuevo and many of the buildings are yet to be restored, but there are some impressive structures. The ruins of

KEY

1 Temple of the Bearded Man.
2 The Great Ballcourt.
3 Temple of Jaguars.
4 Tzompantli or the Platform of the Skulls; nearby Platform of the Eagles and Jaguars.
5 Temple of Chacmool.
6 Ceremonial walkway to Sacred Cenote.
7 El Castillo.
8 Temple of the Warriors.
9 Group of the Thousand Columns.
10 The Market.
11 Xtoloc Cenote.
12 The Tomb of the High Priest or the Ossuary.
13 Temple of the Deer.
14 The Red House.
15 The Observatory—"El Caracol."
16 To the Nunnery and La Inglesia.

LEFT: *Bird's eye view of Chichen Nuevo showing major points of interest.*

the Temple of the Four Lintels has the only known dated inscription within Chichen Itza, which corresponds to July 13, 878. Many of the major structures in Old Chichen can be found in what is termed the Principal Group of the Southwest, including the rebuilt Temple of the Three Lintels that was originally completed around A.D. 879, and the Jaguar Temple that celebrates the prowess of the Jaguar warrior class.

THE SPLENDORS OF CHICHEN NUEVO

Visitors to the altogether more impressive Chichen Nuevo are first greeted by El Castillo, an impressive 82-foot-high (25m), four-sided edifice that is also known as the Pyramid of Kukulcan. The structure is actually built over an older pyramid of the

Maya Post-Classic Period and clearly shows the cross-fertilization of ideas between the Maya and Toltecs. Archaeologists have acknowledged that steep-sided El Castillo closely resembled Pyramid B, the Temple of Quetzalcoatl, at Tula. It also contains stairway carvings depicting the Toltec feathered serpent Quetzalcoatl and doorway carvings that are clearly representations of Toltec warriors.

Despite its warlike Spanish name, the pyramid is actually the Mayan calendar revealed in stone. Each of its faces has 91 steps that together with the single step on each face needed to reach the upper platform bring the total to 365, the number of days in the year. The pyramid also has nine terraces and each is divided in two by the steps thus making a grand total of 18, which also happens to be the number of 20-day months in the Mayan year. The Mayan calendar cycle is also represented by the 52 panels found on the nine

ABOVE: *The Temple of the Warriors and the Group of a Thousand Columns lies to the east of the Kukulcan pyramid.*

LEFT: *The Mayan culture developed in the Yucatan peninsula around 2600 B.C. and by A.D. 250. had expanded to encompass present day southern Mexico, northern Belize, western Honduras, and Guatemala.*

PAGES 140–141: *Another overview of Chichen Nuevo.*

terraces. El Castillo was also placed with great accuracy as it also has astrological significance. At sunrise during the spring and autumn equinoxes, the rounded terraces catch the light and the shadows produced cast a stylized moving serpent-shaped shadow on the northern staircase. The older Temple of Chacmool deep in the bowels of El Castillo is thought to have been built around A.D. 800. It contains a red jaguar throne with inlaid eyes and jade decoration. There is also a reclining statue, a Chacmool, of the rain god Chac that shows the deity with its head turned sideways and holding a plate for either an offering or sacrifice. As this and other sites reveal, It was not uncommon for later rulers to boast of their power by building new temple-pyramids over those of their predecessors.

A little to the northwest of El Castillo lies the *Gran Juego de Pelota* (The Great Ballcourt). Although there are several other such courts dotted across Chichen Itza, this is by far the largest and most impressive of them. Measuring some 479 feet (146m) long by a little over 121 feet (37m) wide, the playing area is flanked by two tall parallel walls that are dotted with cemented stone rings positioned high up. Temples were built at the northern and southern ends of the court. That at the northern end is known as the *Templo del Barnado* (Temple of the Bearded Man) after a carving found there, while that to the south is the *Templo de los Jaguares y Escudos* (Temple of the Jaguars and Shields).

The Maya ball game involved two teams that had to keep a 7–11lb (3–5 kg) rubber ball off the ground using only the players' elbows, hips, knees, and shoulders. The aim was to score points by putting the ball through the stone rings placed high up on the parallel walls. The game was much more than a mere entertainment as it had symbolic and religious meanings. It is thought to have been symbolic of the fighting between good and evil and that the ball was a representation of the sun. Games were

ABOVE: *Statue of Chacmool in front of the ruins of the Temple of the Warriors. The statue is actually an altar and the tray on his stomach was probably used to display* offerings of incense and human hearts following the blood sacrifice.

THIS PAGE: *The Temple of the Warriors is surrounded by hundreds of columns carved with reliefs. More columns have still to be rescued from the clinging grasp of the verdant jungle.*

also sometimes the preliminary to rites of great importance to the Maya and it is thought that on such occasions the members of the winning team were decapitated and honored with deification.

Two platforms that are typical of the fusion between Mayan and Toltec architecture are positioned a little to the east of the ballcourt. The first is known as *Tzompantli* or the *Plataforma de los Craneos* (Platform of the Skulls) because of the carvings of skulls that decorate the platform's walls that also show horrific images of blooded skulls struck together one on top of the other. The T-shaped platform was probably used to display the skulls of sacrificial victims, particularly prisoners and enemies of the Maya. The second platform, the *Plataforma de las Aguilas y los Jaguares* (Platform of the

Eagles and Jaguars) had an equally grisly significance, one hinted at by carvings that show eagles ripping open men's chests to devour their hearts. Experts believe that the platform was probably part of a temple dedicated to the Mayan warrior castes who were responsible for capturing sacrificial victims from other tribes. An additional religious site, the *Templo de Chacmool*, is located a little to the east of these two sites and consists of a platform decorated with a feathered serpent holding a human head in its mouth. Other carvings portray various stars and planets, especially Venus, and show some of their movements.

A little to the north of the temple, a stone road runs for some 330 yards (302m) before reaching the *Cenote Sagrado* (Sacred Cenote), the natural sunken well that played a key part in Chichen Itza's

religious life. The well is something like 213 feet (65m) in diameter and around 115 feet (35m) deep. The well has proved to be a treasure trove of Mayan artifacts and also helped archaeologists gain a greater understanding of religious life in the city-state. It was first dredged in the opening decade of the twentieth century by Edward Thompson, a Harvard professor and the U.S. consul in Yucatan, and he found, among other items, highly decorative gold and jade jewelry from not only all regions of Mexico but also from as far away as distant Colombia. Thompson also recovered human bones and later research work in the 1920s and 1930s and beyond confirmed that the well was used in sacrifices that involved people of all ages and both sexes. The Maya believed that the rain god Chac lived beneath the well's

LEFT: *Front view of the Temple of the Warriors. Its hundreds of pillars are elaborately carved in bas relief some of which retain their original color. Inside elaborate murals once adorned the walls.*

ABOVE: *Part of the Group of a Thousand Columns that stands a little way to the south and east of the Temple of the Warriors. Archaeologists have not been fully able to reveal its purpose.*

ABOVE: *The Great Ball Court is 45ft (13m) wide and 225ft (68.5m) long, with two 25ft (8m) high walls, and halfway along each wall is a stone hoop. After a fiercely contested game the losing captain would lop off the winning captain's head. With this dubious honor the winner would go straight to heaven, rather than have to make the thirteen steps Mayans believed were necessary to get there.*

RIGHT: *The rules of the game are long forgotten but it was probably played between two teams to settle a dispute or to appease the gods. Players could only hit the ball with their elbows, wrists, knees, or hips in an attempt to get it through the hoop.*

Stone hoop placed high up on the wall of the Ballcourt.

surface and regular blood-letting had to be made to placate him.

There is a large complex of buildings to the east of El Castillo, including three smaller ballcourts. There is the *Templo de los Guerros* (Temple of the Warriors), which once comprised numerous carved columns supporting a long-gone roof. There are also several free-standing statues, including two large feathered serpents, a number of animal deities, and what is undoubtedly the city-state's best preserved representations of the rain god Chac. The site, which shows considerable Toltec influence and closely resembles a structure at Tula, was associated with ritual sacrifice. Archaeologists believe that the table within the temple was used in the extraction of sacrifices' hearts. The Temple of the Warriors was built over an earlier structure, the Temple of Chacmool, which was uncovered in 1926.

The *Grupo de Mil Columnas* (Group of a Thousand Columns) stands a little way to the south and east of the Temple of the Warriors but archaeologists have not been fully able to reveal its purposes, although it seems like to have had either a civic or religious function—or possibly both. Excavations have revealed a sophisticated drainage system that channelled rain water into a storage facility on the site's northeast side. The remains of a Mayan bathhouse, the *Bano de Vapor*, lie a little to the south of the garden of columns. An underground heating system and a network of drains have been revealed, and evidence suggests that the building was used in ritual purification ceremonies.

The southern part of Chichen Itza also contains several buildings of religious significance. First, there is the *Tumba del Gran Sacerdote* (High Priest's Grave), which

LEFT: *One of the relief stone carvings on the side of the Ballcourt.*

ABOVE: *The Maya were master mathematicians and were able to calculate the movements of the stars with precision and draw up incredibly accurate star charts. In addition the Maya invented the calendar and devised the only true native American writing system. Many of their buildings are aligned with the heavens.*

RIGHT: *El Castillo or the Kukulcan pyramid was built so that at the vernal equinox the sun would cast a shadow that looks like a serpent writhing down the stepped sides of the pyramid. The pyramid is 197ft (60m) wide by 79ft (24m) high and anyone speaking from the temple at the top can easily be heard at ground level. But anyone there shouting back will instead be answered by a piercing shriek from the echo—the Mayan temple at Tikal also responds the same way.*

is also known as *El Osario* (The Ossuary). Although the pyramid is ruined, archaeologists have been able to discover that it is a Mayan structure and shows no Toltec Influences. Carving of feathered serpents stand guard at the bases of its staircases and a natural cave extends some 50 feet (15.2m) from the interior of the pyramid into the ground. The human bones and various offerings in the form of jewels, gold, and silver found in the cave are believed to have belonged to the city-state's most important priests.

The next significant site in the southern part of the city is a building the Spanish named *El Caracol* (The Snail) because of its spiral staircases. It is one of the very few circular buildings in Chichen Itza and consists of a pair of rectangular platforms with staircases aligned to the west and two circular towers. It was actually constructed as an observatory and the slits in the dome can be aligned with certain planets at certain times of the year as well as the cardinal points of the compass. The observatory was of immense important to the Maya as priests used the dome's mechanism to identify the right time to conduct various practices, such a

celebrations, planting seed and harvesting crops.

A further two large structures lie at the southern end of the city. The first and largest was mistakenly named the *Edificio de las Monjas* (The Nunnery) by the Spanish conquistadores because of its numerous small rooms. The large Maya-style building is certainly imposing, measuring some 197 feet (60m) long, 98 feet (30m) long, and 65 feet (20m) high. Archaeologists have concluded that so imposing a structure was most likely the home of a high priest. The Spanish also misnamed another nearby building as *La Inglesia* (The Church). It is certainly one of the oldest buildings in Chichen Itza and shows both Mayan and Toltec influences in its construction and very ornate decoration.

Archaeologists believe that the final building of note in this southern group of buildings is, in part, among the oldest in Chichen Itza. The *Akab-Dzib* is some 65 yards (59 m) east of the *Edificio de las Monjas* and its name is Mayan for Obscure Writing, which commemorates some hieroglyphs carved into a lintel above a door on the building's south side that have as yet defied decyphering. The oldest of

ABOVE: *The Kukulcan pyramid has 91 steps on each of the four sides—making 364 in total, plus the platform at the top, 365—the number of days of the solar calendar. Each side has 18 terraces—for the number of months in the Mayan year, making a total of 52, the number of years in one Mayan calendar cycle.*

LEFT: These incredible buildings were constructed without the use of metal tools, the wheel, or even beasts of burden to help lift and move the massive stone blocks.

ABOVE: Detail of the terracing on the great Temple of Kukulcan. Kukulcan is the Mayan name for the Mesoamerican god Quetzalcoatl and great stone sculptures of this feathered serpent deity run down either side of the northern staircase. This pyramid temple is built on top of an earlier version which can be reached via a doorway at the base of the pyramid. Hidden deep inside at the top of a steep climb is King Kukulcan's carved stone Jaguar Throne.

the building's seventeen rooms, which also contain obscure writing, date from the second or third centuries A.D.

CHICHEN ITZA'S RECENT HISTORY

The city was largely in ruins when the Spanish conquistadores set foot in Mexico in the second decade of the sixteenth century and, although it is mentioned in numerous documents during the colonial period, no attempts were made to conduct an academic study of Chichen Itza until the nineteenth century. The first thorough study of the city was published in book form in 1841 but it lacked intellectual rigor. Matters improved when the Carnegie Institute of Washington DC explored the site between 1924 and 1936. Today Mexican archaeologists are actively involved on a long-term research and restoration program.

Chichen Itza is a tourist magnet and is best avoided at certain times of the day and year. It is prudent to visit earlier in the day to avoid the crowds of tourists and it is advisable to avoid the spring and autumn equinoxes altogether as crowds flock there in the tens of thousands. There is an admission price except on Sundays and holidays and Chichen Itza is open from 8am to 6pm. Other facilities include a museum, video center, and a couple of bookstores. Visitors should also note that they are not allowed to climb on any of Chichen Itza's structures with the exception of El Castillo.

RIGHT: *Nineteenth century books of adventure and discovery such as Frederick Catherwood's* Voyage to the Yucatan *spread stories of the Mayan civilization. This illustration is the "Pyramid of Kukulcan" by John Lloyd Stephens from Catherwood's book.*

ABOVE: *On September 21 and March 21 (the fall and vernal equinoxes) the sun on the northern steps of El Castillo throws a shadow that looks like a serpent wriggling down the steps, at the base is the carved head of a snake making the illusion complete. In spring the snake moves down the temple and in fall it climbs upward.*

LEFT: *Aerial view of El Caracol, which means "the snail" and refers to the spiral staircase in the side of the observatory.*

ABOVE: *The T-shaped Platform of the Skulls was probably used to display the skulls of sacrificial victims, particularly prisoners and enemies of the Maya.*

RIGHT: *The four entrance ways of El Caracol face the points of the compass and the windows point towards the southernmost and northernmost positions on the horizon where the planet Venus rises. The platforms and terraces of the observatory were built to catch various important celestial events sacred to Kukulcan, the feathered-serpent god of the wind and learning—such as the path of the sun at the time of the vernal and autumnal equinoxes.*

PHOTO CREDITS

All the computer-generated artwork in this book was produced by Robin Pereira from a variety of online and written resources.

All the photographs came from Corbis—thanks to Katie Johnston. Specific credits are as follows:

4	Danny Lehman/Corbis	84	Kevin Schafer/Corbis	158	Bill Ross/Corbis
5	Eye Ubiquitous/Corbis	85	Wolfgang Kaehler/Corbis	159	Francesco Venturi/Corbis
6–7	Macduff Everton/Corbis	86–87	Massimo Mastrorillo/Corbis		
14–15	Tibor Bognar/Corbis	89	Araldo deLuca/Corbis		
20	Kazuyoshi Nomachi/Corbis	90	Alinari Archives/Corbis		
21	Both: Vanni Archive/Corbis	96	Bob Krist/Corbis		
24	Leonard de Selva/Corbis	101	Michael S. Yamashita/Corbis		
30–31	Christie's Images/Corbis	102	John Heseltine/Corbis		
33	Otto Lang/Corbis	103	Carmen Redondo/Corbis		
35	Paul C. Pet/zefa/Corbis	104	Bob Krist/Corbis		
36–37	Randy Faris/Corbis	105	Richard Hamilton Smith/Corbis		
39	Gianni Dagli Orti/Corbis	110–111	George H. H. Huey/Corbis		
42	Neil Beer/Corbis	113	George H. H. Huey/Corbis		
46	Danny Lehman/Corbis	114	George H. H. Huey/Corbis		
47	Bill Ross/Corbis	128	Ric Ergenbright/Corbis		
50	Yann Arthus-Bertrand/Corbis	129	Craig Lovell/Corbis		
51	Nik Wheeler/Corbis	130	Franz-Marc Frei/Corbis		
54–55	Gianni Dagli Orti/Corbis	131	David Muench/Corbis		
56	Nik Wheeler/Corbis	132	Greg Probst/Corbis		
57	Richard A. Cooke/Corbis	133	George H. H. Huey/Corbis		
58–59	Corbis	134–135	Massimo Mastrorillo/Corbis		
69	Yann Arthus-Bertrand/Corbis	142	Danny Lehman/Corbis		
70	Yann Arthus-Bertrand/Corbis	143	Hans Schmied/zefa/Corbis		
71	Yann Arthus-Bertrand/Corbis	144	Macduff Everton/Corbis		
72	Yann Arthus-Bertrand/Corbis	148	Ludovic Maisant/Corbis		
73	ML Sinibaldi/Corbis	149	Ludovic Maisant/Corbis		
74	Paul A. Souders/Corbis	152	Francesco Venturi/Corbis		
75	Eye Ubiquitous/Corbis	153	Macduff Everton/Corbis		
83	Jim Winkley; Ecoscene/Corbis	154	Gianni Dagli Orti/Corbis		

ABOVE: *La Inglesia (the Church) is a small temple dedicated to Chac, the Mayan rain god. His image is carved all over the temple.*

LEFT: *The Mayan civilization was obsessed with death and destruction and there are many gruesome carvings around Chichen Itza, particularly the Platform of the Skulls.*